The Ultimate Air Fryer Baking Cookbook

Discover 100+ Air Fryer Baking Recipes to Satisfy Your Sweet Tooth, Elevate Your Baking Game and Enjoy Mouthwatering Recipes in No time - Cakes, Brownies, Cookies, Breads, and More!

Monica Fisher

Legal Notice:

Copyright 2023 by Monica Fisher- All rights reserved.

This document is geared towards providing exact and reliable information regarding the topic and issue covered. The publication is sold on the idea that the publisher is not required to render an accounting, officially permitted, or otherwise, qualified services. If advice is necessary, legal, or professional, a practiced individual in the profession should be ordered. From a Declaration of Principles which was accepted and approved equally by a Committee of the American Bar Association and a Committee of Publishers and Associations.

Disclaimer Notice:

The information herein is offered for informational purposes solely and is universal as so. The presentation of the information is without a contract or any type of guaranteed assurance. Readers acknowledge that the author is not engaging in the rendering of legal, financial, medical, or professional advice. Please consult a licensed professional before attempting any techniques outlined in this book. The trademarks that are used are without any consent, and the publication of the trademark is without permission or backing by the trademark owner. All trademarks and brands within this book are for clarifying purposes only and are the owned by the owners themselves, not affiliated with this document.

CONTENTS

INTRODUCTION — 9

WHY BAKE IN AN AIR FRYER? — 10

5 TIPS AND TRICKS — 12

5 COMMON MISTAKES — 14

CONCLUSION — 16

AIR FRYER CAKE RECIPES — 17

CHOCOLATE CAKE — 18

SPONGE CAKE — 19

CARROT CAKE — 20

COFFEE CAKE — 21

LEMON RICOTTA CAKE — 22

CARDAMOM CAKE — 23

CRANBERRY CAKE — 24

ORANGE AND KIWI CAKE — 25

TEA CAKE — 26

MANGO CAKE — 27

PLUM CAKE — 28

AIR FRIED CHEESECAKE — 29

LAVA MINI CAKES — 30

RASPBERRY CAKE	31
ORANGE AND CRANBERRY CAKE	32
SEMOLINA ALMOND CAKE	33
APPLE CRUMBLE CAKE	34
CORN CAKE	35
BANANA CAKE	36
STRAWBERRY CAKE	37
BROWNIE RECIPES	38
CHOCOLATE BROWNIES	39
CARAMEL BROWNIES	40
CHEWY BROWNIE	41
MOCHA BROWNIES	42
OREO BROWNIES	43
CHEESE STUFFED BROWNIES	44
CONFETTI BROWNIES	45
LEMON BROWNIES	46
PISTACHIO BROWNIES	47
ZUCCHINI CHOCOLATE BROWNIES	48
NUTELLA BROWNIES	49
CHERRY BROWNIES	50
MINT BROWNIES	51

PEANUT BUTTER BROWNIES	52
ESPRESSO BROWNIES	53
CHOCOLATE FUDGE BROWNIES	54
RED VELVET BROWNIES	55
PUMPKIN BROWNIES	56
S'MORES BROWNIES	57
DULCE DE LECHE BROWNIES	58
AIR FRYER COOKIES	59
CHOCOLATE CHIP COOKIES	60
LEMON COOKIES	61
RED VELVET COOKIES	62
WHITE CHOCOLATE COOKIES	63
GINGER COOKIES	64
COCONUT COOKIES	65
MONSTER COOKIES	66
ROLLED OATS AND RAISINS COOKIES	67
FUNFETTI COOKIES	68
ROCKY ROAD COOKIES	69
BANANA COOKIES	70
AIR FRYER CHAI SPICE COOKIES	71
CARROT COOKIES	72

PEANUT BUTTER AND JELLY COOKIES	73
LEMON BLUEBERRY SHORTBREAD COOKIES	74
MERINGUE COOKIES	75
CARAMEL MACCHIATO COOKIES	76
STRAWBERRY COOKIES	77
LINZER RASPBERRY COOKIES	78
SAMOAN COOKIE	79
AIR FRYER TART AND PIE RECIPES	80
BLUEBERRY PIE	81
BLACKBERRIES PIE	82
RASPBERRY PIE	83
FIG PIE	84
PEACH PIE	85
LEMON TART	86
CHOCOLATE CHIP PIE	87
PLUM PIE	88
CHOCOLATE BROWNIES	89
STRAWBERRY PIE	90
DARK CHOCOLATE PIE	91
APPLE CRANBERRY TART	92
BUTTERMILK TART	93

MIXED BERRIES TART	94
GREEN LIME AND CONDENSED MILK TART	95
MISSISSIPPI MUDTART	96
ORANGE TART	97
ALMOND TART	98
DATES TART	99
WALNUT PEAR TART	100
AIR FRYER BREAD RECIPES	101
OLIVE BREAD	102
ALMOND BREAD	103
PUMPKIN BREAD	104
MOZARELLA BREAD	105
RAISINS BREAD	106
SESAME BREAD	107
CINNAMON BREAD	108
GARLIC BREAD	109
GOAT CHEESE AND AVOCADO BREAD	110
PISTACHIO BREAD	111
MUFFIN AND DONUT RECIPES	112
CARROT WALNUT MUFFINS	113
FIG MUFFINS	114

DATES MUFFINS	**115**
RAISIN MUFFINS	**116**
CREAM MUFFINS	**117**
STRAWBERRY DONUTS	**118**
ALMOND DONUTS	**119**
MATCHA GREEN TEA DONUTS	**120**
COCONUT DONUTS	**121**
BLUBERRY DONUTS	**122**
WHOLE WHEAT DONUTS	**123**
THANKS FOR READING	**124**

INTRODUCTION

Who doesn't adore the smell of bread cooking in a baker's shop while waking in town or the fresh smell of home-baked cookies or biscuits wafting from the kitchen? The scent fills the kitchen and sometimes the whole house, and this is a well-known method used by estate agents to make a house feel more welcoming. However, baking using a conventional oven means having to preheat it in advance, and these days that is expensive with energy prices. It is also very hot in summer heatwaves, and you may be reluctant to turn the oven on just to bake a few cookies but baking in the air fryer can save you both cooking time and money. A few biscuits will bake way faster in an air fryer than in a normal oven. If you are new to baking in an air fryer, here are 5 tips to get you started and 5 of the most common mistakes to avoid.

WHY BAKE IN AN AIR FRYER?

Most people expect to be frying in an air fryer but the heating method is just as convenient for baking. Baking in a conventional oven relies on warm air currents cooking the food evenly. Cooking in an air fryer uses a heating element combined with a fan that circulates the air around the item to be baked. It generally uses less oil and cooks quicker so in these energy-conscious days, baking in your air fryer means you can use it in warmer weather when you do not want the chef to feel as if they are in a sauna in the kitchen.

Making cookies and scones is a simple baking task and you can place them in an ovenproof dish and place them directly into the cooking basket of the air fryer so heavenly smells cook quicker and provide summer treats without heating up the whole house. However, it's not just cookies! In this book you will find so many recipes to try that will have your mouth watering. You can experiment with birthday sponge cakes or fruit cakes depending on the season, you can sweeten some muffins with blueberries or your favourite fruit, you can bake sweetened fruit loaves like banana bread, or you can learn how to make meringues. All of these are possible in your air fryer.

Dessert pies are easy-peasy too in two stages. You can bake the pastry case for a sweet dessert pie simply and quickly in the air fryer, by lining an ovenproof dish with pastry and adding a few dried beans to ensure it does not rise. Then remove it and allow it to cool before adding the sweet filling, which can be baked apple, baked pumpkin, or mixed berries (or any other sweet filling like lemon curd, or raisin and courgette sweet bread), and then just cook it again.

If you like cooking desserts, this is a good way to bake them using the air fryer because you can cook them in stages. For example, if you are making a pie, you can cook the pastry base first, and then the fruit filling. If you want a jam-like consistency, you will need to add sugar and stir them well before baking and then allow them to reach a high temperature. After that, you can add a final layer like a crumble topping. The recipes for crumble can be adapted for whatever fruit you choose.

While the pie is cooking you can mix custard as a topping or add some ice cream or cream to melt on top. Making sweet pies is a perfect use for the bake function of an air fryer.

As you gain experience, your confidence will grow so very soon, you will be using it to bake any homegrown fruit and keep learning so that eventually you can offer spectacular desserts like fruit Pavlova for guests.

Baking for one (or occasionally two) is another reason to use the air fryer so that you do not need to preheat and cook for ages for just one person. Cooking a small cake that you can slice and place in the freezer for when you need it is an option for busy people. It is very simple to buy small oven-proof containers that can fit into the basket tray so that each pot can have different tastes as well. For a busy working cook with plenty of time at weekends, you could save time by preparing several different small desserts and then freezing them for use later in the week after a hard day's work. You will be so glad you did when you re-heat them.

5 TIPS AND TRICKS

1. ***Use your air fryer to bake in summer,*** because it uses only a tiny amount of energy and you do not need to heat a whole oven, just for a few biscuits or a cake. Hot oven cooking in summer is oppressive for the chef so the air fryer method cooks quickly without all that heat escaping into an already warm kitchen.

2. ***Baking in an air fryer happens quicker* than** in a conventional oven so you can reduce the cooking time suggested, unless it is for an air fryer bake. This may mean by as much as 20%, so you will need to check if the baked item is done more frequently too. This makes air frying a better choice environmentally too as you use less energy and less oil. Remember that if you start cooking from a frozen piece of food, it will take defrosting time as well as cooking time. Many recipes give you timing advice for cooking from room temperature or from frozen, so check the recipe and adjust the timing as suggested.

3. ***To check if the baking is ready,*** use a clean knife or skewer and push it into the center of the loaf of bread, cake, or quiche, and examine the skewer when you pull it out. If there is no moisture on the skewer, it usually means it is cooked right through. If it feels slightly wet or moist, give the cake or baked item a few more minutes. Good hygiene will bring success to your baking.

4. ***For easy cleaning,*** you can use an oven-proof container that fits the basket of your air fryer. So if you already have glass containers or cupcake ovenproof pans, these can go straight into your air fryer. Do not fill any containers right to the top with your baking mixture, as it tends to spill if it is too full. The great thing about using ovenproof containers is that they can be popped straight into your dishwasher and no mess.

If you only use the basket tray of the air fryer, then take care of cleaning out any spillages right after they occur. Food that tends to leak can be covered with a layer of aluminum foil or baking foil before cooking to contain them too. These can become extremely hot after baking them, so don't forget to use oven gloves to remove them.

5. ***Easy bakes to start with.*** Cookies are fabulous cooked in the air fryer. Prick them a few times with a fork, and cooking time will be less than usual, so no need to preheat the air fryer. Baked apples and pears will caramelize beautifully in the air fryer and then you can prepare some delicious toppings as they slowly bake. Baked apples or pears make a sweet and healthy dessert that can be topped with cream, ice cream, or yogurt. See some of the fantastic suggestions for desserts in the recipes.

5 COMMON MISTAKES

1. ***Food cooks unevenly.*** You are imagining crispy food but it emerges as a soggy mess. This is mainly caused by using too much oil or baking food that is too wet to start with. Take fruit in sweet sauce in a casserole dish, for example. If you have whole fruit, like an apple or pear and some of that sauce or mixture drips onto the metal parts or the heating element, there will be burns and even smoke. The way to avoid this is to pat off excess oil on food before placing it in the tray or try using aluminum foil under the food to catch any drips. A final method is to try to chop the food to make it the same size so that it cooks at a similar speed although this is difficult for a whole apple. See individual recipes for advice and stick to the temperature and times suggested.

2. ***Setting too high a temperature*** can cause baked food to burn, dry up completely, or only cook on the outside, and nobody wants a cake or cookie that is uncooked in the middle. The best sponge cakes are slightly moist on the inside so you will need to experiment with your air fryer to get it just right. Try not to use a baking tin that is too deep because as I have already said, the food will cook unevenly if it is not turned or moved in the tray and this is not possible with a sponge cake. Keep checking (using that skewer) frequently to see if it is cooked and do not just keep resetting the cooking time without checking if it is done.

3. ***Cookies stick to the basket.*** Experts advise spraying a layer of oil first before adding the cookies or you can add a layer of foil. To avoid burning, you may want to turn them over in the container at least once during the baking time, although if they have chocolate on top, this may prove messy. Adding a cover of aluminum foil will certainly prevent the blackening of the cookies or baked item.

4. ***Overfilling the baking basket.*** Unless you turn the food in the basket several times during the cooking period, the food on the outside will cook better than the food in the middle of the basket. Try to make all food to be baked a similar size and depth so that they all cook at the same pace. This is true of apple rings or cookies. If possible, make the containers a similar size, and if filling the basket tray, do not stuff it to the top! Set the timer for short bakes, then stir or move the food and bake again.

CONCLUSION

Baking in an air fryer offers you the advantage of cooking quicker than in a normal oven and particularly in summer when you do not want the heat from the oven escaping into an already warm kitchen. You use less energy using an air fryer compared to a conventional oven, and meals are healthier with less oil. If your baking dish fits in the basket of your air fryer, you can pop it straight into the dishwasher to save on washing up time too. However, your air fryer will be busy in both summer and winter with these delicious recipes for baked sweet dishes and desserts because they will provide you with ideas to bake food in ways you probably didn't imagine. Your air fryer adds another tool that a good chef can use to bake extraordinary cookies, bread, and delicious pies that suit one person or a family of six. The recipes in this book will add a dessert course to your dinner parties and offer sweet snacks to all your guests.

AIR FRYER CAKE RECIPES

CHOCOLATE CAKE

Servings|4 Time|30 minutes

Nutritional Content (per serving):

Cal |424   Fat |22g   Protein |3.7g   Carbs| 58g   Fibre| 25g

Ingredients:

- 250 grams (1 heap cup) of all-purpose flour
- 125 grams (1/2 cup) unsweetened cocoa powder
- 125 grams (about 1/2 cup) granulated sugar
- 125 grams (about 1/2 cup) of brown sugar
- 2.5 grams (about 1/2 teaspoon) baking powder
- 2.5 grams (about 1/2 teaspoon) of baking soda
- 1 grain (1 pinch) of salt
- 125 ml (about 1/2 cup) of milk
- 125 ml (about 1/2 cup) of vegetable oil
- 2 large eggs
- 5 ml (1 heap teaspoon) of vanilla extract

Directions:

1. Start by preheating your hot air fryer to a temperature of 160° C (325°F).
2. In a large and deep bowl, whisk all together the flour, with the cocoa powder, granulated sugar, brown sugar, baking powder, baking soda, and salt.
3. In a separate bowl, whisk together the fermented milk, vegetable oil, eggs and vanilla extract.
4. Now, pour your wet ingredients into your dry ingredients and stir very well until your ingredients are very well combined.
5. Grease a 6-inch cake pan with cooking spray and pour the batter into the pan.
6. Place the cake pan in the air fryer basket and bake for about 25 to 30 minutes
7. Remove the cake from the air fryer and let it cool in the pan for 10 minutes.
8. Once cooled, remove the cake from the pan and transfer it to a wire rack to cool completely.
9. Serve with your favorite icing or topping.
10. Enjoy your cake!

SPONGE CAKE

Servings|4 Time|30 minutes

Nutritional Content (per serving):

Cal |325   Fat |6g   Protein |3.6g   Carbs| 26g   Fibre| 2g

Ingredients:

- 250 grams (1 heap cup) of all-purpose flour
- 125 grams (about 1/2 cup) unsweetened cocoa powder
- 125 grams (about 1/2 cup) of granulated sugar
- 125 grams (about 1/2 cup) of brown sugar
- 2.5 grams (around 1/2 teaspoon) baking powder
- 2.5 grams (about 1/2 teaspoon) baking soda
- 1 grain (1 pinch) of salt
- 125 ml (about 1/2 cup) of milk
- 125 ml (about1/2 cup) of vegetable oil
- 2 large eggs
- 5 ml (about 1 teaspoon) of vanilla extract

Directions:

1. Preheat your hot air fryer to a temperature of about 160°C (325°F)
2. In a large and deep bowl, whisk together the flour, cocoa powder, granulated sugar, brown sugar, baking powder, baking soda, and salt.
3. In a separate bowl, whisk together the fermented milk, vegetable oil, eggs and vanilla extract.
4. Pour your wet ingredients into your dry ingredients and stir very well until just combined.
5. Grease a 6-inch cake pan with cooking spray and pour the batter into the pan.
6. Place the cake pan in the air fryer basket and bake for about 25 to 30 minutes
7. Remove the cake from your air fryer and let it cool in the pan for 10 minutes.
8. Once cooled, remove the cake from the pan and transfer it to a wire rack to cool completely.
9. Serve with your favorite icing or topping.
10. Enjoy your cake!

CARROT CAKE

Servings|3-4 Time|12 minutes

Nutritional Content (per serving):

Cal |368   Fat |10.6g   Protein |5.9g   Carbs| 35g   Fibre| 1.6g

Ingredients:

- 250 grams (about ½ pound) grated carrots
- 125 grams (about 1/2 cup) all-purpose flour
- 125 grams (1/2 cup) of panko breadcrumbs
- 2.5 grams (about 1/2 teaspoon) paprika
- 2.5 grams (about 1/2 teaspoon) of cumin
- 2.5 grams (about 1/2 teaspoon) of garlic powder
- 2.5 grams (about 1/2 teaspoon) of salt
- 1 large beaten egg

Directions:

1. Preheat your air fryer to a temperature of about 180°C (390°F).
2. In a large and deep bowl, combine the flour, panko breadcrumbs, paprika, cumin, garlic powder and salt.
3. Add in the grated carrots to your dry mixture and stir your ingredients very well.
4. In a small bowl, beat the mixture of the eggs.
5. Form small cakes using your hands; then dip them in the beaten egg.
6. Place the cakes in the air fryer basket.
7. Bake for about 10-12 minutes, until the cakes are golden brown and crispy
8. Serve hot with a sauce of your choice, such as sweet and sour sauce or yogurt sauce.
9. Enjoy your cake!

COFFEE CAKE

Servings|4 Time|20 minutes

Nutritional Content (per serving):

Cal |336   Fat |7g   Protein |8g   Carbs| 38g   Fibre| 2.3g

Ingredients:

- 250 grams (about 1 heap cup) of all-purpose flour
- 125 grams (about 1/2 cup) of granulated sugar
- 30 ml (2 heap tablespoons) of instant coffee
- 5 grams (about 1 teaspoon) of baking powder
- 1 grain (1 pinch) of salt
- 125 ml (about 1/2 cup) of milk
- 30 ml (about 2 tablespoons) of vegetable oil
- 1 Large egg

Directions:

1. Preheat your Air Fryer to a temperature of about 180°C (360°F)
2. In a large and deep bowl, combine all together the flour, the sugar, the instant coffee, the baking powder and the salt.
3. Pour in the milk, vegetable oil and egg to the bowl and stir well until you have a smooth paste.
4. Pour your batter into an appropriately sized cake pan.
5. Place your cake pan in your air fryer basket.
6. Bake for about 15 to 20 minutes, until the cake is golden brown and a toothpick inserted in the center comes out clean.
7. Let the cake cool for a few minutes before unmolding.
8. Serve your cake hot or cold, depending on your preference.
9. Enjoy your cake!

LEMON RICOTTA CAKE

Servings|4 Time|30 minutes

Nutritional Content (per serving):

Cal |369   Fat |15g   Protein |12g   Carbs| 32g   Fibre| 2 g

Ingredients:

- 250 grams (about 1/2 pound) of ricotta
- 200 grams (1 cup) of sugar
- 3 large eggs
- 250 grams (about 1 cup) of all-purpose flour
- 15 grams (1 heap tablespoon) of baking powder
- 1 lemon
- 1 grain (1 pinch) of salt
  15 grams (1 heap tablespoon) of Icing sugar for decoration

Directions:

1. Preheat your Air fryer to about to 180° C (360°F).
2. In a large deep salad bowl, mix all together the ricotta and the sugar until obtaining a homogeneous preparation.
3. Crack in the eggs one at a time, making sure to ix very well after each addition.
4. Grate the lemon zest and add it to the mixture.
5. In a separate deep bowl, combine the flour, the baking powder and 1 pinch of salt.
6. Add in the flour mixture to the ricotta mixture and make sure to mix very well.
7. Pour your mixture into a mold that is suitable for your Air fryer.
8. Place your pan in your preheated air fryer basket and bake for about 25-30 minutes, until the cake is golden brown and a toothpick inserted in the center comes out clean.
9. Let your cake cool for a few minutes before unmolding it
10. Sprinkle with the icing sugar before serving
11. Serve and enjoy your cake!

CARDAMOM CAKE

Servings|3-4Time|25 minutes

Nutritional Content (per serving):

Cal |369   Fat |13g   Protein |13g   Carbs| 26g   Fibre| 2.3g

Ingredients:

- 250 grams (1 heap cup) of all-purpose flour
- 125 grams (1/2 cup) of granulated sugar
- 15 grams (about 1 tablespoon) of ground cardamom
- 1 grain (1 pinch) of salt
- 125 ml (1/2 cup) of milk
- 60 ml (1/4 cup) of vegetable oil
- 1 large egg
- 5 ml (about 1 teaspoon) of vanilla extract
- 2.5 grams (about 1/2 teaspoon) of baking powder

Directions:

1. Preheat your Air fryer to a temperature of about 180°C (360°F)
2. In a large deep bowl, combine all together the flour, the sugar, ground cardamom and the salt.
3. Pour in the milk, the vegetable oil, egg, vanilla extract and baking powder to the bowl and stir very well until you have a smooth batter.
4. Pour your batter into an appropriately sized cake pan.
5. Place your cake pan in your air fryer basket.
6. Bake for about 20 to 25 minutes, or until the cake is golden brown and a toothpick inserted in the center comes out clean.
7. Let your cake cool for a few minutes before unmolding.
8. Serve your cake hot or cold, depending on your preference.
9. Enjoy your cake!

CRANBERRY CAKE

Servings|4-5 Time|20 minutes

Nutritional Content (per serving):

Cal |378   Fat |12g   Protein |6g   Carbs| 15g   Fibre| 1 g

Ingredients:

- 250 grams (1 heap cup) of all-purpose flour
- 125 grams (about 1/2 cup) of sugar
- 15 grams (about 1 tablespoon) of baking powder
- 1 grain (pinch) of salt
- 1 large egg
- 125 ml (about 1/2 cup) of milk
- 60 ml (about 1/4 cup) of vegetable or olive oil
- 250 grams (about ½ pound) of dried cranberries

Directions:

1. Preheat your air fryer to a temperature of about 350°F (180°C).
2. In a large deep bowl, combine all together the flour, with the sugar, the baking powder and the salt.
3. In another bowl, whisk the egg, milk and vegetable oil until the mixture is homogeneous.
4. Pour the liquid mixture over the dry mixture and mix until the batter is smooth.
5. Add the dried cranberries and mix well.
6. Lightly grease the bottom of the air fryer basket with cooking oil.
7. Pour the batter into the basket and spread it evenly.
8. Bake the cranberry cake in your air fryer for about 20 minutes
9. Remove cake from air fryer and let cool before serving.
10. Enjoy your cake!

ORANGE AND KIWI CAKE

Servings|4 Time|20 minutes

Nutritional Content (per serving):

Cal |357   Fat |11g   Protein |7g   Carbs| 33g   Fibre| 1.8 g

Ingredients:

- 250 grams (about 1 cup) of all-purpose flour
- 125 grams (1/2 heap cup) of sugar
- 1 tablespoon baking powder
- 1 grain (1 pinch) of salt
- 1 large egg
- 125 ml (about 1/2 cup) of milk
- 60 ml (about 1/4 cup) of vegetable oil
- 2 large kiwis peeled and diced
- 1 peeled and finely diced oranges

Directions:

1. Preheat your air fryer to 350°F (180°C).
2. In a large and deep bowl, combine the flour, sugar, baking powder and salt.
3. In another bowl, whisk the egg, milk and vegetable oil until the mixture is homogeneous.
4. Pour the liquid mixture over the dry mixture and mix until the batter is smooth.
5. Add the kiwi and orange cubes and mix well.
6. Lightly grease the bottom of the air fryer basket with cooking oil.
7. Pour the batter into the basket and spread it evenly.
8. Bake the Kiwi Orange Cake in the air fryer for about 20 minutes.
9. Remove cake from air fryer and let cool before serving.
10. Enjoy your cake!

TEA CAKE

Servings|4 Time|35 minutes

Nutritional Content (per serving):

Cal |377 Fat |10g Protein |11g Carbs| 25g Fibre| 1.3 g

Ingredients:

- 500 grams (about 2 cups) of all-purpose flour
- 15 grams (1 heap tablespoon) of baking powder
- 1 grain (1 pinch) of salt
- 125 grams (1/2 cup) of unsalted butter, softened
- 250 grams (about 1 heap cup) of granulated sugar
- 2 large eggs
- 125 ml (about 1/2 cup) of milk
- 2 bags of green tea (or your favorite tea)

Directions:

1. Start by preheating your Air fryer to a temperature of 180°C (360°F)
2. In a medium bowl, combine flour, with baking powder and salt.
3. In a large deep bowl, beat the butter and sugar very well together.
4. Add in the eggs, one at a time; making sure to beat very well after each addition.
5. In a small saucepan, heat the milk until it becomes hot but not boiling. Add in the tea bags and let steep for about 5 minutes.
6. Remove the tea bags; then pour in the infused milk to your butter mixture, alternating with the flour mixture, starting and ending with the flour mixture.
7. Pour the batter into a greased and floured 20cm cake tin.
8. Place the cake pan in your air fryer and bake for about 30-35 minutes.
9. Remove cake from air fryer and let cool before serving.
10. Hope you enjoy your Tea Cake!

MANGO CAKE

Servings|4 Time|30minutes

Nutritional Content (per serving):

Cal |315   Fat |9g   Protein |10.3g   Carbs| 27g   Fibre| 0.9g

Ingredients:

- 2 ripe, peeled mangoes
- 2 large eggs
- 50 grams (about 1/4 cup) of granulated sugar
- 50 grams (about 1/4 cup) of all-purpose flour
- 5 grams (about 1 heap) teaspoon of baking powder
- 2.5 grams (about 1/2 teaspoon) of salt
- 60 ml (about 1/4 cup) of vegetable oil

Directions:

1. Start by preheating your Air fryer to a temperature of about 180°C (390°F) in a bowl, whisk the eggs and sugar until the mixture is frothy.
2. Add in the flour, the baking powder and the salt, and mix your ingredients until they become perfectly smooth.
3. Pour in the vegetable oil and mix your ingredients very well again.
4. Finely dice the mangoes; then add them to the batter, make sure stir gently to incorporate your ingredients.
5. Pour your batter into a greased cake pan.
6. Put the pan in your air fryer and bake for a period of about 25 to 30 minutes, or until the cake becomes golden brown and a knife blade comes out clean.
7. Remove your mango cake from your Air Fryer and let cool before serving.
8. Serve and enjoy your delicious mango cake!

PLUM CAKE

Servings|4 Time|30 minutes

Nutritional Content (per serving):

Cal |386   Fat |9g   Protein |12g   Carbs| 23g   Fibre| 1.5g

Ingredients:

- 250 grams (about ½ pound) of flour
- 150 grams (1 ¼ cups) of sugar
- 15 grams (1 heap tablespoon) of baking powder
- 2 large eggs
- 125 ml (about ½ cup) of milk
- 125 ml (about ½ cup) of vegetable oil
- 5 ml (1 heap teaspoon) of liquid vanilla
- 200 grams (about ½ pound) of pitted and halved plums
- 2 heap tablespoons (30 grams) of Icing sugar (for dusting)

Directions:

1. In a large deep bowl, combine all together the flour with the sugar and the baking powder.
2. Add in the eggs, the milk, oil and liquid vanilla, and mix until the batter is smooth.
3. Preheat your air fryer to a temperature of about 180° C (360°F)
4. Pour your batter into a greased round cake tin.
5. Now place the plum halves on top of the batter making sure to press them down slightly.
6. Place your cake pan in the air fryer and bake for about 30 minutes, or until the cake is golden brown and cooked inside.
7. Remove the cake pan from the air fryer and let it cool for about 10 minutes before dusting it with icing sugar.
8. Serve your plum cake warm or cold.
9. Enjoy your cake!

AIR FRIED CHEESECAKE

Servings|4 Time|30 minutes

Nutritional Content (per serving):

Cal |289   Fat |12.5g   Protein |13g   Carbs| 35g   Fibre| 2g

Ingredients:

- 500 grams (about 1 pound) of cream cheese
- 250 grams (1 heap cup) of sugar
- 5ml (1 heap teaspoon) vanilla extract
- 1 tablespoon of flour
- 15 ml (1 heap tablespoon) Olive or coconut oil spray
- 3 large eggs
- 1 heap teaspoon vanilla extract
- 60 ml (about 1/4 cup) of milk
- 60 ml (about 1/4 cup) of sour cream
- 50 grams (around 1/4 cup) of graham cracker crumbs

Directions:

1. In a large and deep bowl, mix all together the cream cheese, with the sugar, flour and vanilla extract until the mixture is smooth.
2. Add in the eggs one at a time, making sure to mix very well after each addition.
3. Add in the milk and sour cream and mix very well.
4. Pour your mixture into a 20cm diameter cake tin, lined with parchment paper.
5. Lightly spray the surface of the cake with olive or coconut oil spray.
6. Place the pan in the hot air fryer preheated to 180°C (365°F) and bake for about 25 to 30 minutes, or until the cake is golden brown and crispy on the outside and firm on the inside.
7. Remove the cake from the pan using parchment paper and let it cool on a wire rack for a few minutes before serving.
8. Sprinkle the surface of cake with graham cracker crumbs before serving if desired.
9. Serve and enjoy your cheesecake!

LAVA MINI CAKES

Servings|6 Time|10minutes

Nutritional Content (per serving):

Cal |335   Fat |10g   Protein |8g   Carbs| 18g   Fibre| 0.3g

Ingredients:

- 125 grams (about ½ cup) of dark chocolate
- 50 grams (about 1/4 cup) of butter
- 2 large eggs
- 50 grams (about1/4 cup) of caster sugar
- 30 grams (3heap tablespoons) of flour
- 1 grain (1 pinch) of salt
- 15 ml (1 heap tablespoon) of olive or coconut oil spray

Directions:

1. Start by melting the dark chocolate and the butter in a bain-marie or in the microwave.
2. In a bowl, beat the eggs and powdered sugar until the mixture is frothy.
3. Add in the flour with 1 pinch of salt to your egg mixture and the powdered sugar and mix very well.
4. Add in the melted chocolate and the butter mixture to your prepared mixture, stirring gently until the mixture is smooth.
5. Lightly spray the cavities of a silicone muffin pan with olive or coconut oil spray.
6. Pour your mixture into the cavities of the muffin tin, filling about two-thirds of each cavity.
7. Place the muffin tin in your air fryer preheated to a temperature of about 180°C (365°F) and bake for about 8-10 minutes, or until the cakes are lightly browned and the surface is firm but the center is still runny.
8. Take the cake out of the air fryer and let it cool for a few minutes before unmolding and serving.
9. Serve and enjoy your lava cake!

RASPBERRY CAKE

Servings|4 Time|25 minutes

Nutritional Content (per serving):

Cal |269   Fat |13g   Protein |10g   Carbs| 26g   Fibre| 0.9g

Ingredients:

- 250 grams (1 heap cup) of all-purpose flour
- 125 grams (about 1/2 cup) of granulated sugar
- 125 grams (about 1/2 cup) of unsalted butter, softened
- 1 large egg
- 5 grams (about 1 teaspoon) of baking powder
- 2.5 grams (about 1/2 teaspoon) of salt
- 60 ml (about 1/4 cup) of milk
- 250 grams (1 heap cup) of fresh or frozen raspberries
- 15 grams (1 heap tablespoon) of powdered sugar for decoration (optional)
- 15 ml (about 1 tablespoon) of olive or coconut oil spray

Directions:

1. Start by preheating your Air fryer to a temperature of about 170° C (350°F)
2. In a large deep bowl, combine all together the flour with the sugar, the baking powder and the salt.
3. Add in the softened butter and work your mixture with a fork or an electric mixer until the mixture is homogeneous.
4. Add in the egg and the milk to your mixture and mix very well.
5. Gently fold your raspberries into the prepared mixture using a spatula.
6. Lightly spray the bottom and sides of your air fryer basket with olive or coconut oil spray.
7. Pour your mixture into the air fryer basket, distributing it evenly.
8. Set the temperature of your air fryer to about 170°C (350°F) and bake the cake for about 20-25 minutes or until golden brown and firm to the touch.
9. Take the cake out of the air fryer and let it cool for a few minutes before unmolding.
10. Sprinkle the cake with powdered sugar before serving.
11. Serve and enjoy your cake!

ORANGE AND CRANBERRY CAKE

Servings|4 Time|30 minutes

Nutritional Content (per serving):

Cal |303   Fat |7.3g   Protein |6.7g   Carbs| 24.6g   Fibre| 0.9 g

Ingredients:

- 125 grams (about 1/2 cup) of softened butter
- 250 grams (about 1 hap cup) of sugar
- 2 large eggs
- 15 grams (about 1 heap tablespoon) of grated orange zest
- 375 grams (about 1 and 1/2 cups) of all-purpose flour
- 12 grams (about 1 1/2 teaspoons) of baking powder
- 2.5 grams (about 1/2 teaspoon) of baking soda
- 1.75 grams (about 1/4 teaspoon) of salt
- 125 ml (about 1/2 cup) of fresh orange juice
- 125 ml (about 1/2 cup) of dried cranberries

Directions:

1. Start by preheating your Air fryer to a temperature of about 180°C (390°F)
2. In a large and deep bowl, whisk the softened butter and sugar until the mixture is creamy.
3. Crack in the eggs one at a time, making sure to beat your ingredients very well after each addition.
4. Add in the grated orange zest and mix very well.
5. In another large and deep bowl, combine all together the flour, with the baking powder, the baking soda and the salt.
6. Add the mixture of the flour to your butter mixture alternately with the orange juice, making sure to start and end with the flour mixture.
7. Mix your ingredients very well after each addition.
8. Add in the dried cranberries and mix gently.
9. Pour your batter into a greased cake pan and smooth it top.
10. Place your pan in your air fryer and bake for about 25 to 30 minutes.
11. Remove the pan from your air fryer and let cool on top of a wire rack before serving.
12. Serve and enjoy your cake!

SEMOLINA ALMOND CAKE

Servings|4Time|20 minutes

Nutritional Content (per serving):

Cal |350   Fat 8g   Protein |13.3g   Carbs| 32g   Fibre| 0.8g

Ingredients:

- 200 grams (about 1 heap cup) of fine semolina
- 250 ml (about 1 cup) of milk
- 250 ml (1 heap cup) of water
- 125 grams (about 1/2 cup) of sugar
- 125 grams (about 1/2 cup) of slivered almonds
- 50 grams (around 1/4 cup) of unsalted butter
- 5 grams (1 heap teaspoon) of almond extract
- 1 grain (1 pinch) of salt
- 15 ml (about 1 tablespoon) of olive or coconut oil spray

Directions:

1. Start by preheating your Air Fryer to a temperature of about 170°C (340° F); then in a medium saucepan, mix all together the semolina, with the milk, water, sugar, slivered almonds, butter and salt.
2. Heat your mixture over a medium heat, making sure to stir constantly, for about 5 minutes or until the semolina has absorbed all the liquid and the mixture thickens.
3. Add in the almond extract to your preparation and mix very well.
4. Lightly spray the bottom and the sides of your air fryer basket with olive or coconut oil spray.
5. Pour your mixture into your air fryer basket, distributing it evenly.
6. Set the temperature of your air fryer to 170°C (350°F) and bake the semolina cake for about 15-20 minutes or until golden brown and firm to the touch.
7. Take your cake out of the air fryer and let it cool for a few minutes before unmolding.
8. Serve the semolina almond cake warm or at room temperature.
9. You can also top the semolina cake with additional slivered almonds and a drizzle of maple syrup or honey.
10. Enjoy your semolina almond cake!

APPLE CRUMBLE CAKE

Servings|3-4 Time|35 minutes

Nutritional Content (per serving):

Cal |296 Fat |12.1g Protein |10.6g Carbs| 13g Fibre| 1.3g

Ingredients:

- 250 grams (1 heap cup) of all-purpose flour
- 5 grams (about 1 teaspoon) of baking powder
- 2.5 grams (about 1/2 teaspoon) of baking soda
- 2.5 grams (about 1/2 teaspoon) of salt
- 125 grams (about 1/2 cup) of unsalted butter, softened
- 125 grams (about 1/2 cup) of sugar
- 2 large eggs
- 2.5 ml (about 1 heap teaspoon) of vanilla extract
- 2 apples, peeled and diced
- 125 ml (about 1/2 cup) of soft caramel
- 15 ml (about 1 tablespoon) of olive or coconut oil spray

Directions:

1. Start by preheating your Air Fryer to a temperature of about 170°C (350°F) in a large deep bowl; combine all together the flour, with the baking powder, baking soda and salt.
2. In another deep bowl, beat the softened butter and the sugar until the mixture becomes light and creamy.
3. Add in the eggs one at a time, making sure to beat very well after each addition.
4. Add in the vanilla extract to your mixture and mix very well.
5. Sift in the flour mixture to your preparation, making sure to mix gently until your preparation becomes homogeneous.
6. Add in the diced apples to your preparation and mix gently to coat them.
7. Lightly spray the bottom and sides of your air fryer basket with olive or coconut oil spray.
8. Pour your prepared mixture into the air fryer basket, distributing it evenly.
9. Pour the soft caramel over the mixture, making circles with a spoon or spatula.
10. Set the air fryer to 170°C (350°F) and bake the cake for about 30-35 minutes or until golden brown and firm to the touch.
11. Take the cake out of the air fryer and let it cool for a few minutes before unmolding.
12. Serve your Apple Caramel Cake warm or at room temperature.
13. Serve and enjoy your cake!

CORN CAKE

Servings|2 Time|30 minutes

Nutritional Content (per serving):

Cal |298   Fat |11.3g   Protein |12 g   Carbs| 29g   Fibre| 1.4g

Ingredients:

- 250 grams (around 1/2 pound) of corn flour
- 250 grams (about ½ pound) of cup all-purpose flour
- 60 grams (about 1/4 cup) of sugar
- 15 grams (1 heap tablespoon) of baking powder
- 1 grain (1 pinch) of salt
- 60 ml (about 1/4 cup) of vegetable oil
- 2 large eggs
- 250 ml (about 1 cup) of milk
- 50 grams (around 1/4 cup) of melted butter
- 15 ml (about 1 tablespoon) of olive or coconut oil spray

Directions:

1. Preheat your Air fryer to a temperature of about 170°C (350°F)
2. In a large deep bowl, combine all together the corn flour, the all-purpose flour, sugar, the baking powder and salt.
3. In another bowl, beat all together the vegetable oil and the eggs.
4. Pour in the milk and melted butter to your mixture and mix your ingredients very well.
5. Add in the flour mixture to your preparation, making sure to mix gently until the preparation is homogeneous.
6. Lightly spray the bottom and the sides of your air fryer basket with the olive or the coconut oil spray.
7. Pour your mixture into your air fryer basket, making sure to distribute it evenly.
8. Set your air fryer to a temperature of about 170° C (350°F) and bake the cake for about 25-30 minutes or until it gets golden brown and firm to the touch.
9. Take your cake out of your air fryer and let it cool for about a few minutes before unmolding.
10. Serve your cornbread cake warm or at room temperature.
11. Enjoy your cake!

BANANA CAKE

Servings|4 Time|12 minutes

Nutritional Content (per serving):

Cal |253   Fat |10g   Protein |11.3g   Carbs| 46g   Fibre| 1g

Ingredients:

- 1 kilogram; 4 ripe bananas (about 2 pounds)
- 125 grams (about 1/2 cup) of all-purpose flour
- 50 grams (about 1/4 cup) of cornstarch
- 50 grams (about 1/4 cup) sugar
- 5 grams (about 1 teaspoon) of baking powder
- 2.5 grams (about 1/2 teaspoon) of salt
- 1 large egg
- 15 ml (1 heap tablespoon) of vegetable oil
- 5 ml (1 heap teaspoon) of vanilla extract

Directions:

1. Start by preheating your air fryer to a temperature of about 200° C (400°F)
2. In a medium deep bowl, combine all together the flour, the cornstarch, the sugar, the baking powder and the salt.
3. In another deep bowl, mash the bananas very well with a fork until it becomes smooth.
4. Crack in the egg, the vegetable oil and the vanilla extract to the bananas and mix very well.
5. Add in the flour mixture to the bananas, making stirring until everything is very well combined.
6. Pour your batter into your air fryer and bake for about 10 to 12 minutes, until the cake becomes golden brown and cooked through.
7. Remove the cake from the air fryer and let them cool on a wire rack for a few minutes before serving
8. Serve and enjoy your cake!

STRAWBERRY CAKE

Servings|3-4 Time|10 minutes

Nutritional Content (per serving):

Cal |255   Fat |13g   Protein |8g   Carbs| 12g   Fibre| 1.5g

Ingredients:

- 200 grams (about 1 cup) of chopped fresh strawberries
- 200 grams (about 1 cup) of all-purpose flour
- 50 grams (about 1/4 cup) sugar
- 5 grams (1 heap teaspoon) of baking powder
- 2.5 grams (about 1/2 teaspoon) of salt
- 1 large egg
- 125 ml (about 1/2 cup) of milk
- 15 ml (1 heap tablespoon) vegetable oil

Directions:

1. Start by preheating your Air fryer to a temperature of about 200° C (400°F).
2. In a medium deep bowl, combine all together the flour, with the sugar, the baking powder and salt.
3. In another deep bowl, beat the egg until they are very well blended.
4. Pour in the milk and the vegetable oil and mix very well.
5. Now, add in the chopped strawberries to your wet ingredients and mix them very well.
6. Sift in the flour mixture with your wet ingredients, making sure to stir very well until your mixture is perfectly combined.
7. Pour your batter into your air fryer and cook for about 8 to 10 minutes, until the cakes become golden brown and cooked through.
8. Remove the cake from your air fryer and let it cool on a wire rack for a few minutes before serving.
9. Serve and enjoy your strawberry cake!
10. These air-fried strawberry cakes are delicious served on their own or with a scoop of vanilla ice cream or homemade whipped cream.
11. Enjoy your cake!

BROWNIE RECIPES

CHOCOLATE BROWNIES

Servings|4 Time| 25 minutes

Nutritional Content (per serving):

Cal |268   Fat |7.9g   Protein |9.8 g   Carbs| 32g   Fibre| 1.5g

Ingredients:

- 125 grams (about 1/2 cup) of all-purpose flour
- 125 grams (about 1/2 cup) of granulated white sugar
- 75 grams (about 1/3 cup) of unsweetened cocoa powder
- 1 grain (1 pinch) of salt
- 60 ml (about 1/4 cup) of vegetable oil
- 2 large eggs
- 5 ml (about 1 teaspoon) of vanilla extract
- 50 grams (about 1/4 cup) of chocolate chips

Directions:

1. Start by preheating your air fryer to a temperature of about 175°C (355°F)
2. In a large deep bowl, combine all together the flour, sugar, cocoa powder and salt.
3. Add in the vegetable oil, eggs and vanilla extract. Mix your ingredients very well until you get a smooth paste.
4. Add in the chocolate chips and mix gently.
5. Pour your prepared batter into a greased brownie pan and place it in the air fryer.
6. Bake your brownies for about 20-25 minutes.
7. Remove the brownie pan from the air fryer and let cool before serving.
8. Serve and enjoy your brownies!

CARAMEL BROWNIES

Servings|4-6 Time|25 minutes

Nutritional Content (per serving):

Cal |321   Fat |6 g   Protein |4g   Carbs| 23g   Fibre| 0.6g

Ingredients:

- 125 grams (about 1/2 cup) of all-purpose flour
- 125 grams (about 1/2 cup) of granulated white sugar
- 75 grams (about 1/3 cup) of unsweetened cocoa powder
- 60 ml (about 1/4 cup) of vegetable oil
- 2 large eggs
- 5 ml (1 heap teaspoon) of vanilla extract
- 50 grams (about 1/4 cup) of chocolate chips
- 60 ml (about 1/4 cup) of caramel sauce
- 1 grain (1 pinch of salt)

Directions:

1. Start by preheating your air fryer to a temperature of about 175°F
2. In a large and deep bowl, combine all together the flour with the sugar, cocoa powder and salt.
3. Add in the vegetable oil, the eggs and the vanilla extract. Mix your ingredients very well until you get a smooth paste.
4. Add in the chocolate chips and mix your ingredients gently.
5. Pour half of the batter you have obtained into a greased brownie pan.
6. Pour the caramel sauce over the dough and spread it evenly.
7. Pour the rest of your batter over the caramel sauce and spread it evenly.
8. Put the brownie pan in your air fryer and bake for about 20 to 25 minutes.
9. Remove the brownie pan from your air fryer and let cool before serving.
10. Serve and enjoy your brownies!

CHEWY BROWNIE

Servings|4-5 Time|25 minutes

Nutritional Content (per serving):

Cal |302   Fat |9.5 g   Protein |10.3g   Carbs| 35g   Fibre| 1.5 g

Ingredients:

- 125 grams (about 1/2 cup) of unsalted butter, cut into pieces
- 250 grams (about 1 heap cup) of granulated white sugar
- 75 grams (about 3/4 cup) of unsweetened cocoa powder
- 2.5 grams (about 1/2 teaspoon) of salt
- 2 large eggs
- 5 ml (about 1 teaspoon) of vanilla extract
- 125 grams (about 1/2 cup) of all-purpose flour
- 2.5 grams (about 1/2 teaspoon) of baking powder
- 60 ml (about 1/4 cup) of milk

Directions:

1. Preheat your Air fryer to a temperature of about 175°C (355°F)
2. In a large deep bowl, melt the butter in a microwave. Add in the sugar, cocoa powder and the salt. Mix your ingredients very well.
3. Crack in the eggs one at a time, mixing very well after each addition. Add in the vanilla extract and mix your ingredients again.
4. Add in the flour and the baking powder and mix very well until the dough is very well combined.
5. Pour in the milk and mix very well until you get a smooth paste.
6. Pour your batter into a greased brownie pan.
7. Place your brownie pan in your air fryer and bake for about 20-25 minutes.
8. Remove the brownie pan from your air fryer and let cool before serving.

MOCHA BROWNIES

Servings|6-8 Time|25 minutes

Nutritional Content (per serving):

Cal |333   Fat |10.6g   Protein |6.9g   Carbs |23g   Fibre |1 g

Ingredients:

- 125 grams (about 1/2 cup) of unsalted butter, cut into pieces
- 250 grams (1 heap cup) of granulated white sugar
- 75 grams (about 3/4 cup) of unsweetened cocoa powder
- 2.5 grams (about 1/2 teaspoon) of salt
- 2 large eggs
- 15 grams (1 heap tablespoon) of instant coffee
- 5 ml (1 heap teaspoon) of vanilla extract
- 125 grams (about 1/2 cup) of all-purpose flour
- 2.5 grams (about 1/2 teaspoon) of baking powder

Directions:

1. Preheat your Air fryer to a temperature of about 175° C (355°F)
2. In a large deep bowl, melt all together the butter in a microwave; then add in the sugar, cocoa powder, salt and instant coffee. Mix your ingredients very well.
3. Crack in the eggs one at a time, mixing very well after each addition; then add in the vanilla extract and mix your ingredients very well again.
4. Add in the flour and the baking powder and mix your ingredients very well until the dough is very well combined.
5. Pour the batter into a greased brownie pan.
6. Place your brownie pan in your air fryer and bake for about 20-25 minutes.
7. Remove your brownie pan from your air fryer and let cool before serving.

OREO BROWNIES

Servings|6 Time|25 minutes

Nutritional Content (per serving):

Cal |298   Fat |10.9g   Protein |8.9g   Carbs| 23.6g   Fibre| 1.5 g

Ingredients:

- 125 grams (about 1/2 cup) of unsalted butter, cut into pieces
- 250 grams (about 1 cup) of granulated white sugar
- 75 grams (about 3/4 cup) of unsweetened cocoa powder
- 2.5 grams (about 1/2 teaspoon) of salt
- 2 large eggs
- 5 ml (about1 heap teaspoon) of vanilla extract
- 125 grams (about 1/2 cup) of all-purpose flour
- 2.5 grams (around 1/2 teaspoon) of baking powder
- 12 Oreos, coarsely chopped

Directions:

1. Start by preheating your Air fryer to a temperature of about 175° C (355°F)
2. In a large deep bowl, melt all together the butter in a microwave. Add in the sugar, cocoa powder and salt. Mix your ingredients very well.
3. Crack in the eggs one at a time, making sure to mix very well after each addition. Add in the vanilla extract and mix again.
4. Sift in the flour and baking powder and mix very well until the dough is very well combined.
5. Add in the chopped Oreos and mix gently.
6. Pour your batter into a greased brownie pan.
7. Place your brownie pan in your air fryer and bake for about 20 to 25 minutes
8. Remove your brownie pan from your air fryer and let your brownies cool before serving.
9. Serve and enjoy your brownies!

CHEESE STUFFED BROWNIES

Servings| 4-6 Time|30minutes

Nutritional Content (per serving):

Cal |301   Fat | 10.3g   Protein |7.3g   Carbs| 25g   Fibre| 1.3g

Ingredients:

- 125 grams (about 1/2 cup) of unsalted butter
- 250 grams (1 heap cup) of granulated white sugar
- 75 grams (about 3/4 cup) of unsweetened cocoa powder
- 2.5 grams (about 1/2 teaspoon) of salt
- 2 large eggs
- 5 ml (1 heap teaspoon) of vanilla extract
- 125 grams (about 1/2 cup) of all-purpose flour

Ingredients for the cheese filling:

- 225 grams (about 1/2 pound) of cream cheese, softened
- 50 grams (about 1/4 cup) of granulated white sugar
- 1 large egg
- 2.5 ml (about 1/2 teaspoon) of vanilla extract

Directions:

1. Start b y preheating your air fryer to a temperature of about 175°C (355°F)
2. In a large deep bowl, melt all together the butter in the microwave. Add in the sugar, the cocoa powder and the salt. Mix your ingredients very well.
3. Crack in the eggs one at a time, making sure to mix very well after each addition.
4. Add in the vanilla extract and mix very well again.
5. Add the flour and mix until the dough is well combined.
6. Pour the batter into a greased brownie pan.
7. In another deep bowl, whisk all together the cream cheese, the sugar, the egg and the vanilla extract until everything becomes smooth.
8. Spoon the cheese filling over your brownie batter.
9. Use a fork to swirl the cream cheese into the brownie batter.
10. Place your brownie pan in your air fryer and bake for about 25-30 minutes or until the brownie is set and the top is lightly browned.
11. Remove the brownie pan from your air fryer and allow it to cool before cutting into squares and serving.
12. Serve and enjoy your brownies!

CONFETTI BROWNIES

Servings| 6 Time|25minutes

Nutritional Content (per serving):

Cal | 269   Fat | 11.3g   Protein |10g   Carbs| 23g   Fibre| 1.5g

Ingredients:

- 125 grams (about 1/2 cup) of unsalted butter, melted
- 250 grams (about 1 cup) of granulated white sugar
- 2 large eggs
- 5 ml (1 heap teaspoon) of vanilla extract
- 125 grams (about 1/2 cup) of all-purpose flour
- 125 grams (about 1/2 cup) of unsweetened cocoa powder
- 2.5 grams (about 1/2 teaspoon) of salt
- 125 grams (about 1/2 cup) of multicolored confetti

Directions:

1. Preheat your air fryer to a temperature of about 175°C (355°F)
2. In a large deep bowl, stir all together the melted butter and the sugar until everything is very well combined.
3. Add the eggs one at a time, making sure to mix very well after each addition. Add in the vanilla extract to your ingredients and mix very well again.
4. In another deep bowl, mix all together the flour, the cocoa powder and salt.
5. Add in your dry ingredients to the butter and the sugar mixture, mixing until everything is very well combined.
6. Stir in the multicolored confetti into your brownie batter.
7. Pour your batter into a greased brownie pan.
8. Place your brownie pan in your air fryer and bake for about 20-25 minutes or until the brownie is set and the top is lightly browned.
9. Remove the brownie pan from your air fryer and allow it to cool before cutting into squares and serving.
10. Serve and enjoy your brownies!

LEMON BROWNIES

Servings| 6 Time|20 minutes

Nutritional Content (per serving):

Cal | 287   Fat | 4g   Protein |5g   Carbs| 28.6g   Fibre| 1g

Ingredients:

- 125 grams (about 1/2 cup) of unsalted butter
- 125 grams (about 1/2 cup) of granulated sugar
- 125 grams (about 1/2 cup) of brown sugar
- 2 large eggs
- 5 ml (1 heap teaspoon) of vanilla extract
- 250 grams (1 heap cup) of all-purpose flour
- 2.5 grams (about 1/2 teaspoon) of salt
- 2.5 grams (about 1/2 cup) of cocoa powder
- 1 Grated lemon zest (about 1 lemon)
- 60 ml (about 1/4 cup) of milk
- 60 ml (about 1/4 cup) of lemon juice

Directions:

1. Preheat your Air Fryer air fryer to a temperature of about 175° C (350° F).
2. In a medium deep bowl, combine all together the flour, salt, cocoa powder and the grated lemon zest.
3. In another deep bowl, beat the butter, with the granulated sugar and brown sugar very well for a few minutes.
4. Add in the eggs one at a time, making sure to beat very well after each time you add an egg in.
5. Add in the vanilla extract and mix very well.
6. Add the flour mixture to your butter mixture and mix until your ingredients are very well incorporated.
7. Pour in the milk and the lemon juice to your mixture and mix very well.
8. Pour your brownie batter into a greased 8x8 inch pan.
9. Place your pan in the air fryer and bake for about 20 minutes.
10. Let your brownies for a few minutes cool before serving.
11. Serve and enjoy your brownies!

> **Note:**

You can serve these brownies with lemon ice cream or lemon topping.

PISTACHIO BROWNIES

Servings| 4-6 Time|20 minutes

Nutritional Content (per serving):

Cal | 352   Fat | 9g   Protein |6.6g   Carbs| 23g   Fibre| 1.5g

Ingredients:

- 125 grams (about 1/2 cup) of unsalted butter
- 125 grams (about 1/2 cup) of granulated sugar
- 125 grams (about 1/2 cup) of brown sugar
- 2 large eggs
- 5 ml (1 heap teaspoon) of vanilla extract
- 250 grams (about 1 cup) of all-purpose flour
- 2.5 grams (about 1/2 teaspoon) of salt
- 125 grams (about 1/2 cup) of cocoa powder
- 1/2 cup unsalted pistachios, coarsely chopped
  1/4 cup milk

Directions:

1. Preheat your air fryer to a temperature of about 175°C (350°F).
2. In a medium deep bowl, combine all together the flour, with the salt, the cocoa powder and the chopped pistachios.
3. In another deep bowl, beat all together the butter, with the granulated sugar and brown sugar very well together
4. Add in the eggs one at a time, making sure to beat very well after each addition.
5. Add in the vanilla extract and mix very well
6. Add in the flour mixture to your butter mixture and mix very well until your ingredients are very well incorporated.
7. Pour in the milk to your mixture and mix very well.
8. Pour your brownie batter into a greased 8x8 inch pan.
9. Place the pan in your air fryer and bake for about 20 minutes
10. Let cool before serving.
11. Serve and enjoy your brownies!

ZUCCHINI CHOCOLATE BROWNIES

Servings| 6 Time|20 minutes

Nutritional Content (per serving):

Cal | 298   Fat | 10.8g   Protein |9g   Carbs| 18.9g   Fibre| 1.7g

Ingredients:

- 1 medium zucchini, finely grated
- 2 large eggs
- 100 grams (about 1/2 cup) of sugar
- 120 grams (about ½ cup) of flour
- 50 grams (1/4 cup) of unsweetened cocoa powder
- 2.5 grams (about 1/2 teaspoon) of baking powder
- 125 ml (about 1/2 cup) of vegetable oil
- 5 ml (about 1 teaspoon) of vanilla extract
- Icing sugar (optional)
- 1 grain (1 pinch) of salt

Directions:

1. Start by preheating your Air fryer to a temperature of about 180°C (370°F)
2. In a large deep bowl, whisk all together the eggs and the sugar until the mixture becomes smooth.
3. Add in the grated zucchini, the flour, the cocoa powder, salt, baking powder, vegetable oil and the vanilla extract.
4. Mix all of your ingredients very well together.
5. Pour your batter into an already prepared oiled brownie pan and bake in your air fryer for about 20 minutes.
6. Let your brownie cool before dusting with icing sugar (optional).
7. Serve and enjoy your brownies!

NUTELLA BROWNIES

Servings| 6 Time|15 minutes

Nutritional Content (per serving):

Cal | 298   Fat | 12g   Protein |10.3g   Carbs| 25g   Fibre| 1.7g

Ingredients:

- 250 ml (1 heap cup) of Nutella
- 125 grams (about 1/2 cup) of all-purpose flour
- 2 large eggs
- 5 ml (1 heap teaspoon) of vanilla extract
- 2.5 grams (about 1/2 teaspoon) of salt
  1/4 cup toasted hazelnuts, chopped (optional)

Directions:

1. Preheat your hot air fryer to a temperature of about 180° C (390°F).
2. In a large deep bowl, whisk all together the Nutella, the flour, the eggs, the vanilla extract and the salt all together until it becomes smooth.
3. If you are using toasted hazelnuts, you can add them now and mix your ingredients again very well.
4. Pour your mixture into an already greased cake pan and place in your air fryer to bake for about 15 minutes, or until the edges are lightly browned and the center is perfectly set.
5. Remove your pan from the air fryer and allow the brownies to cool before serving.
6. Serve and enjoy your brownies!

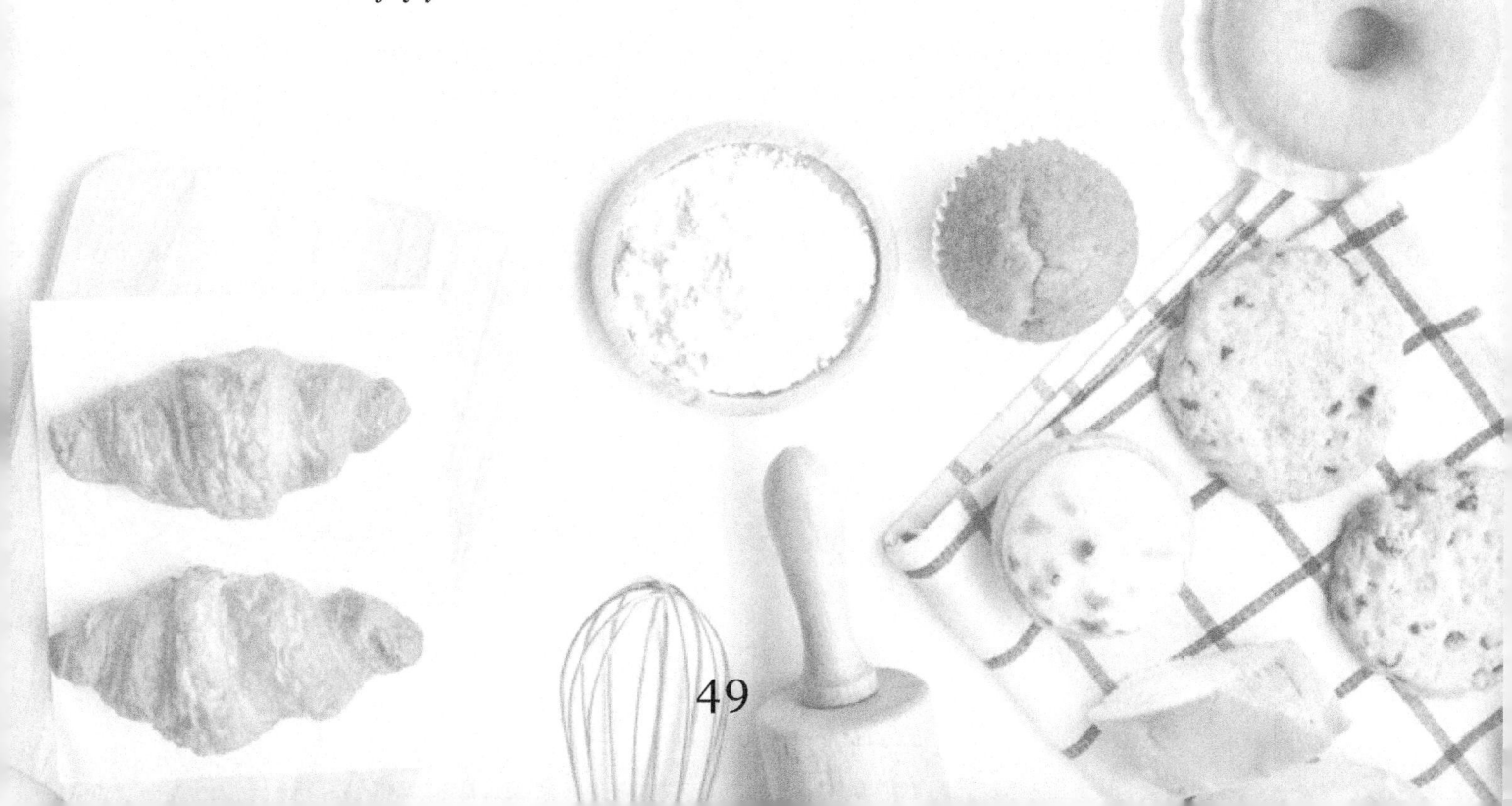

CHERRY BROWNIES

Servings| 6-8   Time|25 minutes

Nutritional Content (per serving):

Cal | 265   Fat | 13g   Protein |10.3g   Carbs| 24g   Fibre| 1.9g

Ingredients:

- 125 grams (about 1/2 cup) unsalted butter
- 250 grams (1 heap cup) of powdered sugar
- 2 large eggs
- 5 ml (1 heap teaspoon) of vanilla extract
- 125 grams (about 1/2 cup) of all-purpose flour
- 30 grams (about 1/3 cup) of cocoa powder
- 1 grain (1pinch) of salt
- 1.5 grams (about ¼) of teaspoon baking powder
- 250 grams (about 1/2 pound) of fresh pitted cherries

Directions:

1. Start by preheating your air fryer to a temperature of about 180° C (390°F)
2. In a large deep bowl, beat all together the butter with the sugar together until your mixture becomes smooth.
3. Add in the eggs and the vanilla extract and beat very well again until your mixture is smooth.
4. In another deep bowl, combine all together the flour, with the cocoa powder, salt and baking powder.
5. Add the flour mixture to your butter mixture, making sure to stir until your ingredients are very well incorporated.
6. Add in the pitted cherries and mix your ingredients again very well.
7. Pour your mixture into a greased cake pan and place in your air fryer for about 20-25 minutes, or until the edges are lightly browned and the center is cooked through.
8. Remove your pan from your air fryer and let your brownies cool before slicing into squares and serving.
9. Serve and enjoy your brownies!

MINT BROWNIES

Servings| 4-6 Time|25 minutes

Nutritional Content (per serving):

Cal | 299   Fat | 12g   Protein |11.3g   Carbs| 26g   Fibre| 1.2g

Ingredients:

- 125 grams (about 1/2 cup) of unsalted butter
- 250 grams (1 heap cup) powdered sugar
- 2 large eggs
- 2.5 ml (about 1/2 teaspoon) mint extract
- 125 grams (about 1/2 cup) of all-purpose flour
- 30 grams (about 1/3 cup) of cocoa powder
- 1.25 grams (about 1/4 teaspoon) of salt
- 1.25 grams (about 1/4 teaspoon) of baking powder
- 125 grams (about 1/2 cup) of dark chocolate chips

Directions:

1. Preheat your Air fryer to a temperature of about 180°C (390°F).
2. In a large and deep bowl, beat all together the butter and the sugar together very well.
3. Crack in the eggs and the Mint extract and beat it again until your mixture is homogeneous.
4. In another deep bowl, combine the flour, cocoa powder, salt and baking powder.
5. Add in the flour mixture to butter mixture, making sure to stir very well until your ingredients are very well incorporated.
6. Add in the dark chocolate chips and mix again very well.
7. Pour your mixture into a greased cake pan and place it in your air fryer for about 20-25 minutes, or until the edges are lightly browned and the center is cooked through.
8. Remove your pan from your air fryer and allow your brownie cake to cool before serving.
9. Serve and enjoy your brownies!

PEANUT BUTTER BROWNIES

Servings| 6 Time|25 minutes

Nutritional Content (per serving):

Cal | 298   Fat | 13g   Protein |8g   Carbs| 24g   Fibre| 1.9g

Ingredients:

- 125 grams (about 1/2 cup) unsalted butter
- 125 grams (about 1/2 cup) of creamy peanut butter
- 250 grams (1 heap cup) of powdered sugar
- 2 large eggs
- 5ml (1 heap teaspoon) of vanilla extract
- 125 grams (about 1/2 cup) of all-purpose flour
- 30 grams (about 1/3 cup) of cocoa powder
- 1 grain (1 pinch) of salt
- 1.25 grams (about 1/4 teaspoon) of baking powder

Directions:

1. Start by preheating your air fryer to a temperature of about 180°C (390°F)
2. In a large deep bowl, beat all together the butter with the peanut butter and the sugar together for a few minutes until your ingredients are very well incorporated.
3. Crack in the eggs and vanilla extract and beat again until your mixture is smooth.
4. In another deep bowl, combine all together the flour, with the cocoa powder, the salt and the baking powder.
5. Add the flour mixture to your butter mixture, stirring until everything is very well incorporated.
6. Pour your mixture into a greased cake pan and place in your air fryer for about 20 to 25 minutes; or until the edges are lightly browned and the center is cooked through.
7. Remove your pan from your air fryer and allow your brownie cake to cool before serving.
8. Enjoy your brownies!

ESPRESSO BROWNIES

Servings| 8   Time|25 minutes

Nutritional Content (per serving):

Cal | 289   Fat | 13g   Protein |8g   Carbs| 18g   Fibre| 1.8g

Ingredients:

- 125 grams (about 1/2 cup) of unsalted butter
- 250 grams (about 1 cup) of powdered sugar
- 2 large eggs
- 15 ml (about 1 heap tablespoon) of espresso powder
- 125 grams (about 1/2 cup) of all-purpose flour
- 30 grams (about 1/3 cup) of cocoa powder
- 1 grain (1 pinch) of salt
- 1.25 grams (about 1/4 teaspoon) of baking powder
- 125 grams (about 1/2 cup) of dark chocolate chips

Directions:

1. Preheat your air fryer to a temperature of about 180°C (390°F)
2. In a large deep bowl, beat all together the butter and the sugar until your mixtures becomes smooth.
3. Add in the eggs and the espresso powder and beat again until your mixture is perfectly homogeneous.
4. In another deep bowl, combine all together the flour, the cocoa powder, salt and baking powder.
5. Add in the flour mixture to your butter mixture, while stirring until everything is very well incorporated.
6. Add in the dark chocolate chips and mix very well again.
7. Pour your mixture into a greased cake pan and place in your air fryer for about 20-25 minutes, or until the edges are lightly browned and the center is perfectly cooked through.
8. Remove your pan from your air fryer and allow your brownie cake to cool before serving.
9. Cut your brownies into squares; then serve and enjoy it!

CHOCOLATE FUDGE BROWNIES

Servings| 6 Time|25 minutes

Nutritional Content (per serving):

Cal | 321   Fat | 11g   Protein |8.6g   Carbs| 32g   Fibre| 1.3g

Ingredients:

- 200 grams (about ½ pound) of dark chocolate
- 100 grams (about 1 cup) of butter
- 150 grams (about ½ cup) of sugar
- 3 large eggs
- 80 grams (about 1/4 cup+ 2 tablespoons of) flour
- 5 grams (1 heap teaspoon) baking powder
  1 grain (about 1 pinch) of salt

Directions:

1. Start by preheating your Air Fryer to a temperature of about 180°C (390°F) and prepare a baking tray lined with parchment paper.
2. In a large and heavy saucepan, melt all together the chocolate and butter over low heat. Make sure to stir regularly to prevent the mixture from burning.
3. In a large deep bowl, whisk all together the eggs and the sugar until the mixture whitens and becomes foamy.
4. Add in the flour, the baking powder and pinch of salt to the egg mixture and stir very well until the batter becomes smooth.
5. Pour your melted chocolate mixture into a deep bowl containing the batter and mix very well.
6. Pour your batter into the prepared pan and place it in your preheated Ai Fryer.
7. Bake the brownies for about 20 to 25 minutes until cooked to your liking. You can also check if they are cooked by sticking a toothpick in the center. If it comes out clean, the brownies are done.
8. Remove your brownies from the Air fryer and let them cool before cutting them into squares and serving them.
9. Serve and enjoy your fudge brownies!

RED VELVET BROWNIES

Servings| 6-8 Time|25 minutes

Nutritional Content (per serving):

Cal | 285   Fat | 8.8g   Protein |9g   Carbs| 24g   Fibre| 1g

Ingredients:

- 125 grams (about 1/2 cup) of unsalted butter
- 250 grams (1 cup) of white sugar
- 2 large eggs
- 30 ml (2 heap tablespoons) of milk
- 15 ml (1 heap tablespoon) of white vinegar
- 15 ml (about 1 heap tablespoon) of red food coloring
- 5 ml (1 heap teaspoon) of vanilla extract
- 250 grams (1 heap cup) all-purpose flour
- 50 grams (about 1/4 cup) of cocoa powder
- 1 grain (1 pinch) of salt
- 1.25 grams (about ¼ teaspoon) of baking soda
- 1.25 grams (about ¼ teaspoon) of baking powder
- 125 grams (about 1/2 cup) of white chocolate chips

Directions:

1. In a large deep bowl, mix all together the melted butter and sugar until the mixture is creamy.
2. Crack in the eggs; then pour in the milk, vinegar, the red food coloring and vanilla extract. Whisk well until the mixture is smooth.
3. In another large and deep bowl, combine the flour, cocoa powder, salt, baking soda and baking powder.
4. Add the flour mixture to the mixture of the butter and mix very well.
5. Add in the white chocolate chips and mix very well until your ingredients are very well incorporated.
6. Preheat your Air fryer to a temperature of about 180° C (390°F)
7. Pour your prepared brownie batter into a brownie pan or a pan suitable for your air fryer.
8. Place your pan in your air fryer and bake for about 20 to 25 minutes, or until the edges are golden brown and the center is cooked through.
9. Remove the pan from your air fryer and allow the brownie to cool completely before cutting it into squares and serving.
10. Serve and enjoy your red velvet brownies!

PUMPKIN BROWNIES

Servings| 6-8   Time|25 minutes

Nutritional Content (per serving):

Cal | 259   Fat | 8.9g   Protein |9.3g   Carbs| 28g   Fibre| 1.2g

Ingredients:

- 120 ml (1/2 cup) pumpkin puree
- 120 ml (1/2 cup) melted butter
- 200g (1 cup) white sugar
- 1 egg
- 5 ml 1 teaspoon vanilla extract
- 120 grams (1 cup) all-purpose flour
- 25 g (1/4 cup) unsweetened cocoa powder
- 2.5 g (1/2 teaspoon) baking soda
- 1.5 g (1/2 teaspoon) ground cinnamon
- 1.5 g (1/4 teaspoon) tsp salt
- 90 g (1/2 cup) semi-sweet chocolate chips

Directions:

1. In a large deep bowl, mix the pumpkin puree, the melted butter, sugar, egg and vanilla extract until the mixture is homogeneous.
2. In another large and deep bowl, combine the flour, the cocoa powder, the baking soda, ground cinnamon and the salt.
3. Sift in the flour mixture to your pumpkin mixture and mix very well.
4. Add in the chocolate chips and mix very well until everything is very well incorporated.
5. Preheat your Air fryer to a temperature of about 180°C (390°F).
6. Pour your brownie batter into a brownie pan or a pan suitable for your air fryer.
7. Place your pan in your air fryer and bake for about 20 to 25 minutes, or until the edges are golden brown and the center is cooked through.
8. Remove the pan from your air fryer and allow the brownie to cool completely before cutting it into squares and serving.
9. Serve and enjoy your brownies!

S' MORES BROWNIES

Servings| 6 Time|20 minutes

Nutritional Content (per serving):

Cal | 314   Fat | 10.5g   Protein |6.3g   Carbs| 27g   Fibre| 1.5g

Ingredients:

- 250 grams (1 heap cup) of all-purpose flour
- 125 grams (about 1/2 cup) of cocoa powder
- 2.5 grams (about 1/2 teaspoon) of salt
- 2.5 grams (about 1/2 teaspoon) of baking powder
- 125ml (about 1/2 cup) of unsalted butter, melted
- 250 grams (1 heap cup) of sugar
- 2 large eggs
- 5 ml (1 heap teaspoon) of vanilla extract
- 250 grams (1 heap cup) chocolate chips
- 250 grams (about 1 heap cup) of miniature marshmallows
- 250 grams (about 1 heap cup) of crumbled graham crackers

Directions:

1. Start by preheating your air fryer to a temperature of about 180°C (390°F).
2. In a large deep bowl, combine all together the flour, cocoa powder, salt and baking powder.
3. In another deep bowl, mix all together the melted butter and the sugar until the mixture is creamy.
4. Crack in the eggs one at a time, making sure to mix very well after each addition.
5. Add in the vanilla extract and mix very well.
6. Add the flour mixture to the butter mixture and mix very well until everything is very well combined.
7. Add in the chocolate chips.
8. Pour half the batter into your air fryer and sprinkle the crumbled graham crackers and miniature marshmallows over the top.
9. Pour in the rest of the batter on top.
10. Bake for about 20 minutes until the top becomes golden and the pastry is cooked.
11. Leave to cool before cutting into pieces and serving.
12. Serve and enjoy your brownies!

DULCE DE LECHE BROWNIES

Servings| 6 Time|25 minutes

Nutritional Content (per serving):

Cal | 43   Fat | 1g   Protein |1.8g   Carbs| 7.4g   Fibre| 1.5g

Ingredients:

- 125 grams (about 1/2 cup) of unsalted butter
- 250 grams (1 heap cup) of sugar
- 2 large eggs
- 5 ml (1 heap teaspoon) of vanilla extract
- 70 grams (about 3/4 cup) of all-purpose flour
- 125 grams (about 1/2 cup) of cocoa powder
- 2.5 grams (about 1/2 teaspoon) of salt
- 125 ml (about 1/2 cup) of Dulce de Leche

Directions:

1. Preheat your Air fryer to a temperature of about 180° C (390°F)
2. In a deep and large saucepan, melt in the butter over a medium heat until it is perfectly melted and begins to foam.
3. Add in the sugar and mix your ingredients very well.
4. Crack in the eggs one at a time, making sure to mix very well after each addition.
5. Add in the vanilla extract and mix your preparation again.
6. In another deep bowl, mix all together the flour with the cocoa powder and the salt.
7. Add in the flour mixture to your butter mixture and mix very well until everything is very well combined.
8. Add in the Dulce de Leche to your batter and mix very well.
9. Pour your batter into your air fryer and bake for about 20 to 25 minutes until the top is golden brown and the batter is perfectly cooked through.
10. Leave to cool before cutting into pieces and serving.
11. Serve and enjoy your brownies!

AIR FRYER COOKIES

CHOCOLATE CHIP COOKIES

Servings| 6 Time|10 minutes

Nutritional Content (per serving):

Cal | 286   Fat | 8.9g   Protein |9.3g   Carbs| 27g   Fibre| 1.5g

Ingredients:

- 125 grams (about 1/2 cup) softened butter
- 125 grams (about 1/2 cup) of granulated sugar
- 50 grams (about 1/4 cup) of brown sugar
- 1 large egg
- 5 ml (1 heap teaspoon) of vanilla extract
- 375 grams (about 1 1/2 cups) of all-purpose flour
- 5 grams (1 heap teaspoon) of baking soda
- 2.5 grams (about 1/2 tsp) of salt
- 250 grams (about 1 heap cup) of chocolate chips
- 15ml (1 heap tablespoon) of non-stick cooking spray

Directions:

1. Start by preheating your Air fryer to a temperature of about 180°C (390°F)
2. In a large deep bowl, beat all together the butter with the granulated sugar very well together.
3. Crack in the egg and vanilla extract and mix until your mixture is very well incorporated.
4. In another deep bowl, combine all together the flour, the baking soda and the salt.
5. Gradually add in the flour mixture to the mixture of the butter, making sure to mix very well until everything is very well incorporated.
6. Add in the chocolate chips and mix your ingredients very well.
7. With the help of a scoop or a tablespoon, drop the balls of dough onto a baking sheet with baking paper or use a baking mat.
8. Lightly spray the dough balls with the use of nonstick cooking spray.
9. Bake your chocolate chip cookies in your air fryer for about 8 to 10 minutes; or until the cookies become golden brown and cooked through.
10. Remove the cookies from your air fryer and let them cool on a cooling rack.
11. Serve and enjoy your cookies!

LEMON COOKIES

Servings| 4-6 Time|10 minutes

Nutritional Content (per serving):

Cal |298   Fat | 10.3g   Protein |7.5g   Carbs| 26g   Fibre| 1.3g

Ingredients:

- 125 grams (about 1/2 cup) of softened butter
- 125 grams (about 1/2 cup) of granulated sugar
- 1 large egg
- 60 ml (about 1/4 cup) of fresh lemon juice
- 15 ml (1 heap tablespoon) of grated lemon zest
- 375 grams (about 1 and 1/2 cups) of all-purpose flour
- 5 grams (1 heap teaspoon) of baking powder
- 1 grain (1 pinch) of salt
- 15 ml (about 1 tablespoon) of non-stick cooking spray

Directions:

1. Preheat your Air fryer to a temperature of about 180°C (390°F).
2. In a large deep bowl, beat all together the butter with the granulated sugar until your mixtures appear smooth.
3. Crack in the eggs, the fresh lemon juice and the grated lemon zest. Mix your ingredients very well until everything is very well incorporated.
4. In another deep bowl, combine the flour with the baking powder and the salt.
5. Gradually add in the flour mixture to the butter mixture, making sure to mix very well until everything is very well incorporated.
6. With the help of a tablespoon, drop the balls of the dough over a baking sheet lined with a parchment paper or a baking mat.
7. Lightly spray your dough balls with nonstick cooking spray.
8. Bake your lemon cookies in your air fryer for about 8 to10 minutes; or until they become golden brown and cooked through.
9. Remove the cookies from your air fryer and let them cool on top of a cooling rack.
10. Serve and enjoy your cookies!

RED VELVET COOKIES

Servings| 4-6 Time|10 minutes

Nutritional Content (per serving):

Cal | 306   Fat | 8.3g   Protein |6.1g   Carbs| 23.5g   Fibre| 0.9g

Ingredients:

- 125 grams (about 1/2 cup) of softened butter
- 125 grams (about 1/2 cup) of granulated sugar
- 1 large egg
- 7 grams (1 heap tablespoon) of red food coloring
- 5 ml (about 1 heap teaspoon) of vanilla extract
- 375 grams (about 1 1/2 cups) of all-purpose flour
- 15 grams (about 2 tablespoons) of unsweetened cocoa powder
- 2.5 grams (about 1/2 teaspoon) of baking soda
- 1 grain (1 pinch) of salt
- 15 ml (1 heap tablespoon) of non-stick cooking spray

Directions:

1. Start by preheating your Air fryer to a temperature of about 180°C (390°F)
2. In a large and deep bowl, beat all together the butter and the granulated sugar very well.
3. Crack in the egg, the red food coloring, and the vanilla extract. Mix your ingredients very well until they are very well incorporated.
4. In another deep large bowl, combine all together the flour, the cocoa powder, baking soda and salt.
5. Gradually add in the flour mixture to your butter mixture, making sure to mix very well until everything is very well incorporated.
6. With the help of a scoop or a tablespoon, drop the balls of the dough onto a baking sheet.
7. Lightly spray your dough balls with nonstick cooking spray.
8. Bake your Red Velvet Cookies in your preheated air fryer for about 8 to 10 minutes; or until they are golden brown and cooked through.
9. Remove the cookies from your air fryer and let them cool on a cooling rack.
10. You can enjoy them as is or add cream cheese frosting on top for a more indulgent result.
11. Serve and enjoy your cookies!

WHITE CHOCOLATE COOKIES

Servings| 6 Time|10 minutes

Nutritional Content (per serving):

Cal | 236   Fat | 6.9g   Protein |7.3g   Carbs| 29g   Fibre| 1.3g

Ingredients:

- 125 grams (about 1/2 cup) of softened butter
- 125 grams (about 1/2 cup) of granulated sugar
- 1 large egg
- 5 ml (about 1 heap teaspoon) of vanilla extract
- 375 grams (about 1 and 1/2 cups) all-purpose flour
- 2.5 grams (about 1/2 teaspoon) of baking soda
- 1 grain (1 pinch) of salt
- 125 grams (about 1/2 cup) of white chocolate chips
- 125 grams (about 1/2 cup) of chopped macadamia nuts
- 15 ml (about 1 heap tablespoon) of non-stick cooking spray

Directions:

1. Start by preheating your Air Fryer to a temperature of about 180°C (390°F)
2. In a large and deep bowl, beat all together the butter and the granulated sugar until the mixture becomes smooth.
3. Add in the egg and the vanilla extract. Mix your ingredients very well until they are very well incorporated.
4. In another deep bowl, combine all together the flour, with the baking soda and the salt.
5. Gradually sift in the flour mixture to your butter mixture, making sure to mix very well until everything is very well incorporated.
6. Add in the white chocolate chips and the chopped macadamia nuts and mix very well.
7. With the help of a scoop or tablespoon, drop the balls of dough onto a baking sheet or a baking mat.
8. Lightly spray the dough balls with the use of nonstick cooking spray.
9. Bake the white chocolate macadamia nut cookies in your air fryer for about 8 to 10 minutes; or until your cookies are golden brown and cooked through perfectly.
10. Remove your cookies from your air fryer and let them cool on a cooling rack.
11. Serve and enjoy your cookies!

GINGER COOKIES

Servings| 6 Time|10 minutes

Nutritional Content (per serving):

Cal **315**   Fat | 6.8g   Protein |7.3g   Carbs| 18.9g   Fibre| 0.8g

Ingredients:

- 125 grams (about 1/2 cup) of softened butter
- 125 grams (about 1/2 cup) of brown sugar
- 50 grams (1/4 cup) of molasses
- 1 large egg
- 450 grams (about 1 pound) of all purpose flour
- 7 grams (1 heap tablespoon) of ground ginger
- 5 grams (about 1 heap teaspoon) of ground cinnamon
- 2.5 grams (around 1/2 teaspoon) of baking soda
- 1 grain (1 pinch) of salt
- 15 ml (about 1 tablespoon) of non-stick cooking spray

Directions:

1. Preheat your air fryer to a temperature of about 180°C (390°F)
2. In a large deep bowl; then beat all together the butter, with the brown sugar and the molasses very well
3. Crack in the egg and mix your ingredients very well.
4. In another deep bowl, combine all together the flour, the ground ginger, ground cinnamon, the baking soda and the salt.
5. Gradually add the flour mixture to your butter mixture, mixing until everything is very well incorporated.
6. With the use of a scoop or tablespoon, drop balls of your dough onto a baking sheet with baking paper or a baking mat.
7. Lightly spray your dough balls with the use of nonstick cooking spray.
8. Bake your gingerbread cookies in your air fryer for about 8 to 10 minutes; or until they become golden brown and cooked through.
9. Remove the cookies from your air fryer and let them cool on a cooling rack.
10. Serve and enjoy your cookies!

COCONUT COOKIES

Servings| 6 Time|10 minutes

Nutritional Content (per serving):

Cal | 235   Fat | 11.3g   Protein |10.8g   Carbs| 15g   Fibre| 1.2g

Ingredients:

- 500 grams (about 1 pound) of shredded coconut
- 100 grams (about 2/3 cup) of sugar
- 50 grams (about 1/4 cup) of all-purpose flour
- 1 grain (1 pinch) of salt
- 2 large eggs
- 5 ml (1 heap teaspoon) of vanilla extract
- 30 ml (about 2 tablespoons) of melted coconut oil

Directions:

1. Preheat your air fryer to a temperature of about 180°C (390°F).
2. In a large deep bowl, combine all together the coconut, the sugar, flour and the salt.
3. In another deep bowl, beat all together the eggs and add in the vanilla extract and the melted coconut oil. Mix your ingredients very well until they become smooth.
4. Add the egg mixture to your coconut mixture and stir very well until everything is very well combined.
5. Form balls of dough about 1 tablespoon each and place them on a baking sheet lined with parchment paper.
6. Place the baking sheet in your air fryer and bake for about 8 to10 minutes, or until the cookies are golden brown.
7. Remove the brownies from your Air fryer and let them cool on a wire rack.
8. Once cooled, serve and enjoy your coconut cookies!

MONSTER COOKIES

Servings|6 Time|10 minutes

Nutritional Content (per serving):

Cal |299   Fat |13g   Protein |6g   Carbs| 24g   Fibre| 1.3 g

Ingredients:

- 100 grams (about ½ cup) of softened butter
- 100 grams (about ½ cup) of brown sugar
- 1 large egg
- 2.5 ml (about 1/2 teaspoon) of vanilla extract
- 140 grams (about ¼ pound) of all-purpose flour
- 2.5 grams (about 1/2 teaspoon) of baking soda
- 1 grain (1 pinch ¼ of salt=
- 50 grams (1/4 cup) of rolled oats
- 100 grams (1/2 cup) of chocolate chips
- 50 grams (about ¼ cups) of grated coconut
- 50 grams (1/4 cup) of chopped walnuts

Directions:

1. In a large deep bowl, whisk all together the butter and the sugar until everything is perfectly incorporated.
2. Crack in the egg and the vanilla extract and mix very well.
3. In another deep bowl, combine all together the flour with the baking soda and the salt. Add your mixture to your butter mixture and mix very well.
4. Add in the rolled oats, the chocolate chips, the coconut and the chopped walnuts. Mix your ingredients very well so that the ingredients are evenly distributed.
5. Form balls of your dough the size of a golf ball and place them on top of the rack of your air fryer, making sure to space them very well apart.
6. Bake your cookies for about 8 to 10 minutes at a temperature of about 175°C (355°F) in your Air fryer until it becomes golden brown and slightly crispy.
7. Take your cookies out of your air fryer and let them cool on a wire rack.
8. Repeat until all the batter is used.
9. Serve and enjoy your cookies!

ROLLED OATS AND RAISINS COOKIES

Servings|6 Time|10 minutes

Nutritional Content (per serving):

Cal |278   Fat |8.7g   Protein |6.5g   Carbs| 25g   Fibre| 1.3 g

Ingredients:

- 250 grams (about ½ pound) of all-purpose flour
- 2.5 grams (about 1/2 teaspoon) of baking soda
- 1 grain (1 pinch) of salt
- 2.5 grams (about 1/2 teaspoon) of ground cinnamon
- 125 grams (about 1/2 cup) of unsalted butter, softened
- 125 grams (about 1/2 cup) of granulated white sugar
- 125 grams (about 1/2 cup) of brown sugar
- 1 large egg
- 5 ml (about 1 heap teaspoon) of vanilla extract
- 250 grams (about ½ pound) of quick cooking rolled oats
- 125 grams (about 1/2 cup) of raisins

Directions:

1. In a medium deep bowl, combine the flour, the baking soda, the salt and the cinnamon and set your mixture aside.
2. In a large deep bowl, beat all together the butter, the granulated sugar and the brown sugar until the mixture is creamy.
3. Crack in the egg and the vanilla extract and beat your mixture very well.
4. Add in the flour mixture and stir until your ingredients are very well combined.
5. Add in the rolled oats and the raisins and mix your preparation until everything is very well incorporated.
6. Preheat your Air fryer to a temperature of about 175°C (355°F).
7. Form balls of dough about 2.5 cm and place them on the grate of your Air Fryer.
8. Bake your cookies in your Air fryer for about 8 to 10 minutes, or until it becomes golden brown.
9. Remove the cookies from your Air fryer and let them cool on a cooling rack for about 10 minutes before serving.
10. Serve and enjoy your cookies!

FUNFETTI COOKIES

Servings|4 Time|10 minutes

Nutritional Content (per serving):

Cal |278   Fat |13g   Protein |7.2g   Carbs| 18g   Fibre| 0.8g

Ingredients:

- 125 grams (about 1/2 cup) of softened butter
- 125 grams (about 1/2 cup) of sugar
- 1 large egg
- 5 ml (about 1 teaspoon) of vanilla extract
- 375 grams (about 1 1/2 cups) of all-purpose flour
- 2.5 grams (about 1/2 teaspoon) of baking soda
- 1 grain (1 pinch) of salt
- 125 grams (about 1/2 cup) of mixed colored sprinkles

Directions:

1. Start by preheating your air fryer to a temperature of about 180°C (390°F)
2. In a large and deep bowl , beat the butter and sugar until the mixture looks smooth
3. Crack in the egg and the vanilla extract; then mix your ingredients very well.
4. In another bowl, combine the flour, the baking soda and the salt.
5. Add the flour mixture to the mixture of the butter and mix very well until the dough is perfectly smooth.
6. Stir the sprinkles into your batter.
7. Form balls of the dough of about 2 tablespoons each and place them on top of a baking sheet lined with a parchment paper.
8. Place the baking sheet in your air fryer and bake for about 8 to 10 minutes, or until the cookies are golden brown and crispy.
9. Remove the cookies from your air fryer and let them cool on a wire rack.
10. Once cooled, serve and enjoy your delicious Funfetti Cookies!

ROCKY ROAD COOKIES

Servings|6 Time|10 minutes

Nutritional Content (per serving):

Cal |225   Fat |6.5g   Protein |5.3g   Carbs| 26g   Fibre| 1 g

Ingredients:

- 125 grams (about 1/2 cup) of softened butter
- 125 grams (about 1/2 cup) of brown sugar
- 50 grams (about 1/4 cup) of white sugar
- 1 large egg
- 5 ml (1 heap teaspoon) of vanilla extract
- 375 grams (about 1 and 1/2 cups) of all-purpose flour
- 50 grams (about ¼ cup) of unsweetened cocoa powder
- 2.5 grams (about 1/2 teaspoon) of baking soda
- 1 grain (1 pinch) of tsp salt
- 200 grams (about 1 cup) of miniature marshmallows
- 125 grams (about 1/2 cup) of chopped pecans
- 125 grams (about 1/2 cup) of semi-sweet chocolate chips

Directions:

1. Start by preheating your Air fryer to a temperature of about 180°C (390°F).
2. In a large deep bowl; beat all together the butter, the brown sugar and the white sugar for a minute or two
3. Crack in the egg and the vanilla extract; then mix your ingredients very well.
4. In another deep bowl, combine all together the flour, the cocoa powder, the baking soda and the salt.
5. Add in the flour mixture to your butter mixture and mix very well until your dough is smooth.
6. Add in the marshmallows, the pecans, and the chocolate chips to your batter and stir very well until your mixture is very well-combined.
7. Form balls of dough about 2 tablespoons each and place them on a baking sheet lined with parchment paper.
8. Place the baking sheet in your air fryer and bake for about 8 to10 minutes, or until the cookies are golden brown and crispy.
9. Remove the cookies from your air fryer and let them cool on a wire rack.
10. Once cooled, enjoy these delicious Rocky Road Cookies!

BANANA COOKIES

Servings|4 Time|15 minutes

Nutritional Content (per serving):

Cal |236   Fat |7g   Protein |6g   Carbs| 21g   Fibre| 0.9g

Ingredients:

- 2 very ripe bananas
- 160grams (about 1 ¼ cups) of flour
- 50 grams (about ¼ cup) of brown cane sugar or brown sugar
- 100 grams (about ½ cup) of dark chocolate
- 1 heap tablespoon (1 packet) of vanilla sugar
- 15 grams (about 1 heap
- tablespoon) of yeast
- 1 Large egg

Directions:

1. Preheat your Air Fryer to a temperature of about 180° C (390°F)
2. In a large and deep mixing bowl, vigorously mix the egg, brown sugar and vanilla sugar.
3. Add in the flour and baking powder and mix very well again.
4. On a plate, mash the bananas with a potato masher or a fork. Then incorporate it into the preparation.
5. Add the chocolate chips and spread into the cookie dough.
6. On a baking sheet lined with parchment paper, drop spoonful of cookie mix. Space them well because the cookies will spread.
7. Place the cookies in your Air Fryer basket.
8. Bake for about 15 minutes.
9. Remove the cookies from your Air Fryer and let cool for a few minutes.
10. Serve and enjoy your cookies.

AIR FRYER CHAI SPICE COOKIES

Servings|4 Time|20 minutes

Nutritional Content (per serving):

Cal |336   Fat |7g   Protein |8g   Carbs| 38g   Fibre| 2.3g

Ingredients:

- 250 grams (about 1 heap cup) of all-purpose flour
- 125 grams (about 1/2 cup) of granulated sugar
- 125 grams (about 1/2 cup) of softened butter
- 5 grams (1 heap teaspoon) of baking powder
- 5 grams (about 1 heap teaspoon) of ground Chai spices
- 1 grain (1 pinch) of salt
- 1 large egg
- 15 ml (about 1 heap tablespoon) of milk

Directions:

1. Start by preheating your air fryer to a temperature of about 180° C (390°F)
2. In a large and deep mixing bowl, combine all together the flour, with the sugar, baking powder, the ground Chai spices and the salt.
3. Add in the softened butter and mix your ingredients very well.
4. In a small separate bowl, beat all together the egg and the milk together, then add them to your flour mixture and stir very well until you get a dough forms a ball.
5. Divide your dough into small balls and place them in your Air fryer.
6. Bake your cookies for about 10 to 12 minutes.
7. Remove your Air Fried cookies from the air fryer and set aside to cool for 5 minutes.
8. Serve and enjoy your cookies!

CARROT COOKIES

Servings|6-8 Time|12 minutes

Nutritional Content (per serving):

Cal |203   Fat |10g   Protein |9.8g   Carbs| 25g   Fibre| 1.5 g

Ingredients:

- 250 grams (about 1 heap cup of) all-purpose flour
- 125 grams (about 1/2 cup) of white sugar
- 125 grams (about 1/2 cup) of brown sugar
- 1 grain (1 pinch) of salt
- 2.5 grams (about 1/2 teaspoon) of baking soda
- 2.5 grams (about 1/2 teaspoon) of baking powder
- 5 grams (about 1 heap teaspoon) of ground cinnamon
- 2.5 grams (about 1/2 teaspoon) of ground ginger
- 125 ml (about 1/2 cup) of coconut oil, melted
- 2 large eggs
- 5 ml (about 1 heap teaspoon) of vanilla extract
- 250 grams (about 1 heap cup) of grated carrots

Directions:

1. Start by preheating your Air fryer to a temperature of about 180°C (350°F)
2. In a large and deep bowl, combine all together the flour, sugars, salt, baking soda, baking powder, cinnamon and ginger.
3. In another separate bowl, mix the melted coconut oil, eggs and vanilla extract very well.
4. Add the liquid mixture to your dry mixture and mix very well.
5. Add in the grated carrots and mix your ingredients very well until they are very well incorporated.
6. Drop spoonful of the obtained batter over a baking sheet lined with a parchment paper.
7. Put the baking sheet in your air fryer and cook for about 10 to 12 minutes.
8. Set your cookies aside to rest for about 5 minutes.
9. Serve and enjoy your cookies

PEANUT BUTTER AND JELLY COOKIES

Servings|6 Time|12 minutes

Nutritional Content (per serving):

Cal |269   Fat |14g   Protein |11g   Carbs| 13g   Fibre| 1.1g

Ingredients:

- 120 grams creamy peanut butter (1/2 cup)
- 100 grams granulated sugar (1/2 cup)
- 100 grams light brown sugar (1/2 cup)
- 113 grams unsalted butter, softened (1/2 cup)
- 1 large egg
- 5 ml vanilla extract (1 teaspoon)
- 180 grams all-purpose flour (1 1/2 cups)
- 5 grams baking powder (1 teaspoon)
- 2.5 grams of baking soda (1/2 teaspoon)
- 2.5 grams of salt (1/2 teaspoon)
- 160 grams of strawberry jelly (1/2 cup)

Directions:

1. In a large and deep mixing bowl, beat all together the peanut butter, granulated sugar, brown sugar, and butter.
2. Beat in the egg with vanilla extract and mix very well
3. In a separate deep bowl, whisk all together the flour, baking powder, baking soda, and salt.
4. Gradually add in your dry ingredients to your mixture of peanut butter
5. Divide your dough into half and make sure to shape each half into the shape of log.
6. Now, wrap each of the logs into a plastic wrap and refrigerate it for a period of about 30 minutes.
7. Preheat the air fryer to 180°C (350°F).
8. Remove your dough from the refrigerator and cut each log into 1/2-inch (1.25cm) slices.
9. Place half of the slices on the bottom of the air fryer basket, leaving some space between each cookie.
10. Spoon a small dollop of strawberry jelly onto each cookie slice.
11. Top with the remaining jelly
12. Bake your cookies for about 12 minutes; then remove and let it cool for about 10 minutes
13. Serve and enjoy your cookies!

LEMON BLUEBERRY SHORTBREAD COOKIES

Servings|6 Time|12 minutes

Nutritional Content (per serving):

Cal |263   Fat |11g   Protein |6.3g   Carbs| 18g   Fibre| 1.1 g

Ingredients:

- 125 g (1 cup) all-purpose flour
- 60 g (1/4 cup) powdered sugar
- 113 g (1/2 cup) unsalted butter, softened
- The grated zest of a lemon
- 60 g (1/2 cup) fresh or frozen blueberries

For garnishing:

- 50 grams (1/4 cup) powdered sugar
- 30 ml (about 2 heap tablespoons) of lemon juice
- 5 grams (1 heap teaspoon) of cornstarch maizen

Directions:

1. Preheat your air fryer to 180°C (350°F).
2. In a large and deep mixing bowl, combine the flour, sugar and lemon zest.
3. Add in the butter and mix well until the mixture becomes a bit sandy.
4. Add in the blueberries and mix your ingredients gently until they are evenly distributed in the batter.
5. Shape the dough into balls the size of a golf ball and place them on the hot air fryer baking sheet, spacing them 2.5 cm (1 inch) apart.
6. Bake the cookies for about 10 to 12 minutes, or until lightly browned.
7. Meanwhile, prepare the filling by combining the powdered sugar, lemon juice and cornstarch in a small bowl.
8. Once the cookies are cooked, take them out of the air fryer.
9. Serve and enjoy your cookies!

MERINGUE COOKIES

Servings|6 Time|8 minutes

Nutritional Content (per serving):

Cal |236   Fat |6.3.g   Protein |6.3g   Carbs| 27g   Fibre| 1.3 g

Ingredients:

- 125 grams (1 cup) all-purpose flour
- 60grams (1/2 cup) powdered sugar
- 60 grams (1/4 cup) unsalted butter, softened
- 1 medium egg
- 15 grams (1 tablespoon grated lemon zest
- 2.5 grams (about 1/2 teaspoon) baking powder
- 1.25 grams (1/4 teaspoon) of salt

For the meringue:

- 2 egg whites
- 60grams (1/4 cup) powdered sugar

Directions:

1. Preheat your air fryer to 180°C (350°F).
2. In a medium deep bowl, combine the flour, powdered sugar, lemon zest, baking powder and salt.
3. Add in the softened butter and the egg to your prepared dry mixture and mix very well.
4. Using a tablespoon, drop balls of dough onto your air fryer baking sheet. Leave a space of about 2 cm (1 inch) between each cookie.
5. Bake the lemon cookies for 6 about 8 minutes.
6. Remove the cookies from the air fryer and let cool on a wire rack for a few minutes.
7. To make the meringue, whisk the egg whites until they look frothy, then gradually add in the powdered sugar, continuing to whisk for a minute.
8. Place a tablespoon of meringue on each cooled cookie, leaving a small space around the edge.
9. Return your cookies with the meringue to the hot air fryer baking sheet and cook for an additional 2-3 minutes.
10. Remove the cookies from the air fryer and set aside to cool for 5 minutes.
11. Serve and enjoy your cookies!

CARAMEL MACCHIATO COOKIES

Servings|6 Time|10 minutes

Nutritional Content (per serving):

Cal |232   Fat |9.5g   Protein |10.3g   Carbs| 22g   Fibre| 1.23 g

Ingredients:

- 125 grams (1heap cup) of all-purpose flour
- 75 grams (1/3 cup) of powdered sugar
- 15 grams (1 tablespoon) of instant espresso powder
- 1/2 teaspoon of salt
- 1/2 teaspoon baking powder
- 60 ml (1/4 cup) milk
- 1 egg
- 1 teaspoon vanilla extract
- 60 grams (about/4 cup) unsalted butter, softened
- 50 grams (1/4 cup) soft caramel
- Extra powdered sugar for sprinkling

Directions:

1. Preheat your Air fryer to 180°C (350°F).
2. In a large bowl, combine the flour, powdered sugar, instant espresso powder, salt and baking powder.
3. In another large and deep bowl, whisk all together the milk, the egg and vanilla extract.
4. Add the milk mixture to your dry ingredients and mix very well.
5. Add in the softened butter and soft caramel to the bowl and mix well until your batter becomes smooth.
6. Using a tablespoon, form balls of dough and place them in your air fryer.
7. Bake the cookies for 8 to 10 minutes or until golden and slightly crispy.
8. Remove your cookies from fryer and sprinkle with additional powdered sugar.
9. Allow cookies to cool before serving.
10. Serve and enjoy your cookies!

STRAWBERRY COOKIES

Servings|6 Time|10minutes

Nutritional Content (per serving):

Cal |222   Fat |8.9g   Protein |9g   Carbs| 23g   Fibre| 0.8g

Ingredients:

- 125 grams (1/4 pound) of all-purpose flour
- 60 grams (about 1/4 cup) powdered sugar
- 1.25 grams (about 1/4 teaspoon) of salt
- 115 grams (about 1/2 cup) unsalted butter, softened
- 5 ml (1 heap teaspoon) of vanilla extract
- 60 grams (about 1/4 cup) of dried strawberries, finely chopped
- Extra powdered sugar for sprinkling

Directions:

1. Preheat your air fryer to 180°C (350°F).
2. In a large and deep bowl, combine the flour, powdered sugar and salt.
3. Add in the softened butter and vanilla extract to your bowl and stir with a wooden spoon very well.
4. Stir the chopped dried strawberries into the batter and mix your ingredients very well.
5. Using a tablespoon, form balls of dough and place them in your air fryer.
6. Bake your cookies for 8 to 10 minutes or until golden and slightly crispy.
7. Remove the cookies from your air fryer and sprinkle with additional powdered sugar.
8. Set your cookies aside to cool before serving.
9. Serve and enjoy your cookies!

LINZER RASPBERRY COOKIES

Servings|4 Time|10 minutes

Nutritional Content (per serving):

Cal |265   Fat |8.3g   Protein |9.3g   Carbs| 21g   Fibre| 1.2g

Ingredients:

- 125 grams (1 heap cup) all-purpose flour
- 60 grams (about 1/2 cup) ground almonds
- 60 grams (about 1/4 cup) powdered sugar
- 1.25 grams (about 1/4 tsp) of salt
- 115 grams (about 1/2 cup) of unsalted butter, softened
- 1 egg yolk
- 2.5 grams (about 1/2 teaspoon) of vanilla extract
  60 grams (about 1/4 cup) raspberry jam

Directions:

1. Preheat your air fryer to 180° C (350° F).
2. In a large and deep bowl, combine the flour, ground almonds, powdered sugar and salt.
3. Add in the softened butter, the egg yolk and vanilla extract to the bowl and stir with a wooden spoon until the batter becomes perfectly smooth.
4. Form a ball of dough and wrap it in plastic wrap and let refrigerate for about 30 minutes.
5. Using a rolling pin, roll out your dough on a lightly floured surface until it is about 5 mm (1/4 inch) thick.
6. Using a heart-shaped cookie cutter, cut out shapes in your dough; then repeat until your dough is perfectly used up.
7. Place half of the cut shapes on the rack of your air fryer.
8. Using a spoon spread a thin layer of raspberry jam on each shape.
9. Place the remaining shapes on top of the jam to form cookies.
10. Bake the cookies for about 8 to 10 minutes.
11. Remove your cookies from your Air fryer and let them cool on a wire rack.
12. Enjoy your cookies

SAMOAN COOKIE

Servings|6-8 Time|10 minutes

Nutritional Content (per serving):

Cal |235   Fat |8.1g   Protein |10.1g   Carbs| 19g   Fibre| 1.3g

Ingredients:

- 125 grams (1 heap cup) of all-purpose flour
- 60 grams (about 1/2 cup) powdered sugar
- 1.25 grams (about 1/4 tsp) of salt
- 115 grams (about 1/2 cup) of unsalted butter, softened
- 2.5ml (about 1/2 teaspoon) of vanilla extract
- 60 grams (about 1/2 cup) unsweetened grated coconut
- 20 grams (about 1/4 cup) rolled oats
- 1/4 cup soft caramel
- 100 grams (about 3/4 cup) of chocolate chips

Directions:

1. Preheat your air fryer to a temperature of about 180°C (350°F).
2. In a large and deep bowl, combine the flour, powdered sugar and the salt.
3. Add in the softened butter and vanilla extract to the bowl and stir with a wooden spoon until your batter becomes perfectly smooth.
4. Stir the shredded coconut and the rolled oats into your batter and mix very well.
5. Form golf ball sized balls of dough and flatten slightly to form discs.
6. Place the discs of dough on the grid of your air fryer.
7. Bake your cookies for about 8 to 10 minutes.
8. Remove your cookies from the fryer and let them cool on a wire rack.
9. In a microwave-safe bowl, heat the soft caramel for about 20 seconds.
10. Dip the bottom of each cookie in the melted caramel; then place them on a sheet of parchment paper.
11. Melt the chocolate chips in the microwave, stirring every 20 seconds.
12. Pour your melted chocolate over the caramel-covered cookies to form an even layer.
13. Refrigerate your cookies for about 10 to 15 minutes or until the chocolate is completely hardened.
14. Serve and enjoy your cookies!

AIR FRYER TART AND PIE RECIPES

BLUEBERRY PIE

Servings|4 Time|25 minutes

Nutritional Content (per serving):

Cal |268   Fat |5g   Protein |3.9g   Carbs| 29g   Fibre| 1.5g

Ingredients:

- 1 pie crust
- 250 grams (about ½ pound) of fresh blueberries
- 50 grams (about 1/4 cup) of white sugar
- 50 grams (about 1/4 cup) of all-purpose flour
- 15 ml (1 heap tablespoon) lemon juice
- 5 ml (1 heap teaspoon) of lemon zest
- 1.25 grams (about 1/4 teaspoon) of salt

Directions:

1. Preheat your air fryer to 180° C (350° F).
2. Spread the pie dough in a 23 cm (9 inch) pie pan and prick it with a fork.
3. In a large and deep bowl, combine the blueberries, sugar, flour, lemon juice, lemon zest and salt.
4. Pour the blueberry mixture over the pie crust.
5. Place your pie in your air fryer and bake for about 20-25 minutes or until the crust is golden brown and the blueberries are hot and slightly bubbly.
6. Remove your pie from the fryer and let it cool on a wire rack.
7. Serve your blueberry pie warm or cold, accompanied by a scoop of vanilla ice cream if desired.
8. Enjoy your pie!

BLACKBERRIES PIE

Servings|6 Time|25 minutes

Nutritional Content (per serving):

Cal |245   Fat |10g   Protein |9.3g   Carbs| 24g   Fibre| 1.3g

Ingredients:

- 1 pie crust
- 710 ml (about 3 heaps cups) of fresh blackberries
- 120 ml (about 1/2 cup) of white sugar
- 30 ml (2 heap tablespoons) all-purpose flour
- 15 ml (1 heap tablespoon) lemon juice
- 2.5 ml (about 1/2 teaspoon) of lemon zest

Directions:

1. Preheat your air fryer to 180° C (350° F).
2. Spread the pie dough in a 23 cm (9 inch) pie pan and prick it with a fork.
3. In a large and deep bowl, combine the blackberries, sugar, flour, lemon juice, lemon zest.
4. Pour the blackberry mixture over your pie crust.
5. Place your pie in the air fryer and bake for about 20 to 25 minutes or until the crust is golden brown and the blackberries are hot and slightly bubbly.
6. Remove your pie from your Air Fryer and let it cool on a wire rack.
7. Serve your blackberry pie warm or cold, with a scoop of vanilla ice cream if desired.
8. Serve and enjoy your pie!

RASPBERRY PIE

Servings|4 Time|25 minutes

Nutritional Content (per serving):

Cal |278   Fat |6.7g   Protein |7g   Carbs| 23g   Fibre| 1.2 g

Ingredients:

- 1 pie crust
- 480 ml (About 2 cups) of fresh raspberries
- 120 ml (1/2 cup) white sugar
- 30 ml (2 heap tablespoons) cornstarch
- 15 ml (1 heap tablespoon) lemon juice
- 2.5 ml (about 1/2 teaspoon) lemon zest

Directions:

1. Preheat your Air fryer to 180°C (350°F).
2. Spread the pie dough in a 23 cm (9 inch) pie pan and prick it with a fork.
3. In a large and deep bowl, combine the raspberries, sugar, cornstarch, the lemon juice and lemon zest.
4. Pour the raspberry mixture over the pie crust.
5. Place your pie in your air fryer and bake for about 20 to 25 minutes.
6. Remove your pie from your Air Fryer and let it cool on a wire rack.
7. Serve your raspberry pie warm or cold, accompanied by a scoop of vanilla ice cream if desired.
8. Enjoy your pie!

FIG PIE

Servings|4Time|25 minutes

Nutritional Content (per serving):

Cal |270   Fat 7.3g   Protein |3g   Carbs| 39g   Fibre| 1g

Ingredients:

- 1 pie crust
- 6 fresh figs, quartered
- 60 ml (about 1/4 cup) brown sugar
- 15 ml (1 heap tablespoon) honey
- 15 ml (1 heap tablespoon) lemon juice
- 5 ml (1 heap teaspoon) vanilla extract
- 2.5 ml (1/2 teaspoon) ground cinnamon
- 2.5 ml (about 1/2 teaspoon) ground nutmeg
  2.5 ml (about 1/2 teaspoon) salt

Directions:

1. Preheat your air fryer to 180° C (350° F).
2. Spread the pie dough in a 23 cm (9 inch) pie pan and prick it with a fork.
3. In a large and deep bowl, combine the fig wedges, brown sugar, honey, lemon juice, vanilla extract, cinnamon, nutmeg and salt.
4. Pour the fig mixture over your pie crust.
5. Place your pie in your air fryer and bake for about 20 to 25 minutes or until the crust is golden brown and the figs are hot and slightly bubbly.
6. Remove your pie from your Air fryer and let it cool on a wire rack.
7. Serve your fig tart warm or cold, accompanied by a scoop of vanilla ice cream if desired.
8. Enjoy your pie!

PEACH PIE

Servings|4 Time|25 minutes

Nutritional Content (per serving):

Cal |236   Fat |11g   Protein |11g   Carbs| 39g   Fibre| 1.5g

Ingredients:

- 1 pie crust
- 4 peaches, peeled and quartered
- 60 grams (About 1/4 cup) granulated sugar
- 30 ml (2 heap tablespoons) all-purpose flour
- 5 ml (1 heap teaspoon) ground cinnamon
- 2.5 ml (about 1/2 teaspoon) ground nutmeg
- 2.5 ml (about 1/2 teaspoon) salt
- 30 ml (2 heap tablespoons) melted butter

Directions:

1. Preheat your air fryer to about 180°C (350°F).
2. Spread your pie dough in a 23 cm (9 inch) pie pan and prick it with a fork.
3. In a large and deep bowl, combine the peach wedges, granulated sugar, flour, cinnamon, nutmeg and salt.
4. Pour your peach mixture over the pie crust.
5. Drizzle the melted butter over the top of the pie.
6. Place your pie in your Air fryer and bake for about 20 to 25 minutes.
7. Remove the pie from your Air Fryer and let it cool on a wire rack for about 5 minutes.
8. Serve your peach pie warm or cold, accompanied by a scoop of vanilla ice cream if desired.
9. Enjoy your pie!

LEMON TART

Servings|4 Time|25minutes

Nutritional Content (per serving):

Cal |253.6   Fat |6.5g   Protein |3.6 g   Carbs| 32g   Fibre| 0.9g

Ingredients:

- 1 pie crust
- 210 grams (1 heap cup) of granulated sugar
- 60 ml (about 1/4 cup) all-purpose flour
- 4 large eggs
- 180 ml (about 3/4 cup) fresh lemon juice
- 120 ml (about 1/2 cup) milk
- 60 ml (about 1/4 cup) melted butter

Directions:

1. Preheat your air fryer to 180° C (350° F).
2. Spread the pie dough in a 23 cm (9 inch) pie pan and prick it with a fork.
3. In a large and deep bowl, stir together the granulated sugar, all-purpose flour and eggs very well.
4. Add in the fresh lemon juice, milk and melted butter, and mix your ingredients very well.
5. Pour the lemon mixture over the pie crust.
6. Place your pie in your air fryer and bake for about 20 to 25 minutes.
7. Remove the pie from the fryer and set aside to cool on a wire rack for a few minutes.
8. Serve your lemon pie cold, with a splash of whipped cream or grated lemon zest if desired.
9. Serve and enjoy your pie!

CHOCOLATE CHIP PIE

Servings|3-4 Time|25 minutes

Nutritional Content (per serving):

Cal |248   Fat |8.96g   Protein |4g   Carbs| 46g   Fibre| 1.52g

Ingredients:

- 1 pie crust
- 200 grams (1 heap cup) semi-sweet chocolate chips
- 120 ml (about 1/2 cup) creamy peanut butter
- 120 ml (about 1/2 cup) of milk
- 2 large eggs
- 60 grams (about 1/4 cup) granulated sugar
- 30 ml (2 heap tablespoons) all-purpose flour
- 5 ml (about1 heap teaspoon) vanilla extract
- 1 grain (1 pinch) of salt

Directions:

1. Preheat your Air Fryer to a temperature of about 180° C (350° F).
2. Spread the pie dough in a 23 cm (9 inch) pie pan and prick it with a fork.
3. Melt the chocolate chips and peanut butter in saucepan over low heat, stirring constantly.
4. Add in the milk, eggs, granulated sugar, all-purpose flour, vanilla extract and pinch of salt to the chocolate and peanut butter mixture and stir very well.
5. Pour chocolate and peanut butter mixture over pie crust.
6. Place your pie in your preheated air fryer and bake for about 20 to 25 minutes.
7. Remove the pie from the fryer and let it cool on a wire rack.
8. Serve your Chocolate Peanut Butter Pie cold, with a splash of whipped cream.
9. Enjoy your pie!

PLUM PIE

Servings|4Time|30 minutes

Nutritional Content (per serving):

Cal |255   Fat |13g   Protein |8g   Carbs| 12g   Fibre| 1.5g

Ingredients:

- 1 pie crust
- 1 kg (about 2 pounds) plums, pitted and halved
- 60 grams (about 1/4 cup) granulated sugar
- 15 ml (1 heap tablespoon) all-purpose flour
- 5 ml (1 heap teaspoon) ground cinnamon
- 1 grain (1 pinch) of salt

Directions:

1. Preheat your air fryer to 180° C (350° F).
2. Spread the pie dough in a 23 cm (9 inch) pie pan and prick it with a fork.
3. In a large and deep bowl, combine the plums, granulated sugar, all-purpose flour, ground cinnamon and pinch of salt.
4. Arrange the plum mixture on the pie crust.
5. Place your pie in your air fryer and bake for about 25 to 30 minutes or until the crust is golden brown and the plums are tender.
6. Remove the pie from the fryer and let it cool on a wire rack.
7. Serve your plum pie cold, with a scoop of vanilla ice cream or whipped cream if desired.
8. Serve and enjoy your pie!

CHOCOLATE BROWNIES

Servings|4 Time| 30minutes

Nutritional Content (per serving):

Cal |264.3   Fat |6.31g   Protein |6.2 g   Carbs| 37.3g   Fibre| 1.6g

Ingredients:

- 1 pie crust
- 4 pears, peeled, cored and quartered (1/2 pound)
- 60 grams (about 1/4 cup) granulated sugar
- 30 ml (2 heap tablespoons) all-purpose flour
- 5 ml (1 heap teaspoon) vanilla extract
- 5 ml (1 heap teaspoon) ground cinnamon
- 1 grain (1 pinch) of salt

Directions:

1. Preheat your Air fryer to 180°C (350°F).
2. Spread the pie dough in a 23 cm (9 inch) pie pan and prick it with a fork.
3. In a large and deep bowl, combine the pear wedges, granulated sugar, all-purpose flour, vanilla extract, ground cinnamon and pinch of salt.
4. Arrange the pear mixture on the pie crust.
5. Place your pie in the air fryer and bake for about 25-30 minutes.
6. Remove the pie from the fryer and let it cool on a wire rack.
7. Serve your pear pie cold, accompanied by a scoop of vanilla ice cream or whipped cream if desired.
8. Enjoy your pear pie

STRAWBERRY PIE

Servings|4 Time|30 minutes

Nutritional Content (per serving):

Cal |235.3   Fat |5.8g   Protein |4.65g   Carbs| 39.5g   Fibre| 0.8g

Ingredients:

- 1 pie crust (broken or puff pastry)
- 200 grams (about 1/2 pound) of rhubarb, cut into chunks
- 200 grams (about 1/2 pound) strawberries, halved
- 50 grams (about ¼ cup) of sugar
- 15 grams (about 1 heap tablespoon) of cornstarch
- 1 large beaten egg

Directions:

1. Preheat your air fryer to a temperature of about 180° C (350° F).
2. Spread your pie dough in a 20 cm (8 inch) diameter pie pan and prick it with a fork.
3. In a deep mixing bowl, combine the rhubarb sections, strawberries, sugar and cornstarch.
4. Pour the fruit mixture over your pie crust.
5. Brush the edges of your pie crust with the beaten egg.
6. Place your pie in your air fryer and bake for about 25 to 30 minutes.
7. Set your pie aside to cool before serving.
8. Enjoy your pie!

DARK CHOCOLATE PIE

Servings|4 Time|20 minutes

Nutritional Content (per serving):

Cal |223.1   Fat |10.2g   Protein |8.54g   Carbs| 29g   Fibre| 0.9 g

Ingredients:

- 150 grams (about 1 cup) all-purpose flour
- 25 g (about 1/4 cup) unsweetened cocoa powder
- 100 g (about 1/2 cup) granulated sugar
- 100 grams (around 1/2 cup) unsalted butter, at room temperature
- 1 large egg
- 5 ml (about 1 heap teaspoon) of vanilla extract
- 150 grams (1 heap cup) of chocolate chips

Directions:

1. Preheat your air fryer to about 175°C (350°F).
2. In a large and deep bowl, mix all together the flour, cocoa and sugar.
3. Add in the butter, egg and vanilla extract and mix very well.
4. Spread your dough in a greased pie pan and prick it in several places with a fork.
5. Spread the chocolate chips over your dough.
6. Place your pie in the air fryer and bake for about 15-20 minutes.
7. Remove your pie from the air fryer and set it aside to cool before serving.
8. Serve and enjoy your pie!

APPLE CRANBERRY TART

Servings|4 Time|25 minutes

Nutritional Content (per serving):

Cal |199.3   Fat |9.5g   Protein |8g   Carbs| 26.9g   Fibre| 0.9 g

Ingredients:

- 1 pie crust (broken or puff pastry)
- 2 apples peeled, cored and thinly sliced
- 100 grams (about 3/4 cup) dried cranberries
- 50 grams (about 1/4 cup) sugar
- 15 grams (1 heap tablespoon) of flour
- 2.5 grams (about 1/2 teaspoon) of ground cinnamon
- 1.25 grams (about 1/4 teaspoon) ground nutmeg
- 1 grain (1 pinch) of salt
- 25 grams (about 2 heap tablespoons) of melted butter

Directions:

1. Preheat your air fryer to 180° C (350° F).
2. In a large and deep bowl, combine the apples, cranberries, sugar, flour, cinnamon, nutmeg and salt.
3. Roll out the pie crust and place it in the bottom of an air fryer compatible pie pan.
4. Pour the apple mixture over the pie crust.
5. Drizzle the melted butter over the apples.
6. Place your pie pan in the air fryer and bake for 20-25 minutes.
7. Remove the pie pan from the air fryer and set aside to cool for a few minutes before serving.
8. Serve and enjoy your delicious apple and cranberry tart!

BUTTERMILK TART

Servings|4 Time|30 minutes

Nutritional Content (per serving):

Cal |278   Fat |11.5g   Protein |9.32g   Carbs| 27g   Fibre| 0.9 g

Ingredients:

- 1 pie crust (broken or puff pastry)
- 240 ml (1 heap cup) buttermilk
- 100 grams (about 1/2 cup) sugar
- 30 grams (2 heap tablespoons) of flour
- 15 ml (about 1 heap tablespoon) of lemon juice
- 1 grain (1 pinch) of salt
- 2 large eggs
- 30 ml (about 2 heap tablespoons) of melted butter

Directions:

1. Preheat your air fryer to 180°C (350°F)
2. In a large and deep bowl, combine the buttermilk, sugar, flour, lemon juice and salt.
3. Crack in the eggs one at a time; make sure to mix your ingredients very well after each addition.
4. Add in the melted butter and mix very well until your dough becomes smooth.
5. Roll out your pie crust and place it in the bottom of your air fryer compatible pie pan.
6. Pour the buttermilk mixture over your pie crust.
7. Place your pie pan in the air fryer and bake for about 25-30 minutes.
8. Remove your tart pan from your air fryer and set it aside to cool for a few minutes before serving.
9. Serve your buttermilk tart warm or at room temperature, with a scoop of vanilla ice cream or whipped cream.
10. Serve and enjoy your tart!

MIXED BERRIES TART

Servings| 4 Time|30minutes

Nutritional Content (per serving):

Cal |255   Fat | 9.5g   Protein |8.3g   Carbs| 32g   Fibre| 1.1 g

Ingredients:

- 1 pie crust (broken or puff pastry)
- 400 grams (about 4 cups) frozen mixed berries (strawberries, blueberries, raspberries, etc.)
- 100grams (about 1/2 cup) sugar
- 30 grams (about 2 tablespoons) cornstarch
- 15 ml (about 1 heap tablespoon) of lemon juice
- 2.5 ml (about 1/2 teaspoon) of vanilla extract
- 1.25 grams (about 1/4 tsp) of salt

Directions:

1. Preheat your air fryer to 180° C (350° F).
2. In a large and deep bowl, combine all together the mixed berries, sugar, cornstarch, lemon juice, vanilla extract and salt.
3. Roll out the tart crust and place it in the bottom of your air fryer compatible tart pan.
4. Pour the mixed berry mixture over the tart crust.
5. Place the tart pan in your air fryer and bake for about 25-30 minutes.
6. Remove your tart pan from your air fryer and set it aside to cool for a few minutes before serving.
7. Serve your mixed berry tart warm or at room temperature, with a scoop of vanilla ice cream or whipped cream.
8. Enjoy your tart!

GREEN LIME AND CONDENSED MILK TART

Servings| 4Time|30minutes

Nutritional Content (per serving):

Cal | 269   Fat | 10.2g   Protein |9.3g   Carbs| 25.6g   Fibre| 1g

Ingredients:

- 1 pie crust (broken or puff pastry)
- 240 ml (about 1 heap cup) fresh lime juice
- 395 grams (1 can) sweetened condensed milk
- 3 egg yolks
- 30 grams (1 heap tablespoon) of grated lime zest
- 2.5 ml (about 1/2 teaspoon) of vanilla extract
- 1.25 grams (about 1/4 tsp) of salt

Directions:

1. Preheat your Air fryer to a temperature of about 180°C (350°F).
2. In a large and deep bowl, combine the lime juice, sweetened condensed milk, egg yolks, grated lime zest, vanilla extract and salt.
3. Roll out the pie crust and place it in the bottom of an air fryer compatible pie pan.
4. Pour the lime mixture over the pie crust.
5. Place your tart pan in your air fryer and bake for about 25-30 minutes.
6. Remove your tart pan from your air fryer and set aside to cool for a few minutes before serving it.
7. Serve your lime tart warm or at room temperature, with a scoop of vanilla ice cream or whipped cream.
8. Serve and enjoy your tart!

MISSISSIPPI MUDTART

Servings| 4 Time|30 minutes

Nutritional Content (per serving):

Cal | 277   Fat | 4.3g   Protein |7.5g   Carbs| 32g   Fibre| 1.5g

Ingredients:

- 1 pie crust (broken or shortbread)
- 150grams (about 2/3 cup) unsalted butter
- 150 grams (about 3/4 cup) powdered sugar
- 60 grams (about 1/2 cup) unsweetened cocoa powder
- 3 large eggs
- 120 ml (about 1/2 cup) milk
- 5 ml (about 1 heap teaspoon) of vanilla extract
- 1.25 grams (about 1/4 teaspoon) of salt
- 100 grams (about 2/3 cup) semi-sweet chocolate chips
- 50 grams (about 1/2 cup) chopped pecans

Directions:

1. Preheat your Air Fryer to 180° C (350° F).
2. In a large heavy saucepan, melt all together the butter over a low heat. Add in the sugar and cocoa powder and mix your ingredients very well.
3. Remove your saucepan from the heat and add in the eggs, make sure to add them one by one; and mix very well every time you add an egg.
4. Add in the milk, vanilla extract and salt, and mix your ingredients very well.
5. Add in the chocolate chips and the chopped pecans and mix very well.
6. Roll out your tart crust and place it in the bottom of your air fryer.
7. Pour your chocolate mixture over the tart crust.
8. Place your tart pan in your air fryer and bake for about 25 to 30 minutes.
9. Remove your pie pan from your air fryer and set aside to cool for a few minutes before serving.
10. Serve your Mississippi Mud tart warm or at room temperature, with a scoop of vanilla ice cream or whipped cream.
11. Serve and enjoy your tart!

ORANGE TART

Servings| 4 Time|35 minutes

Nutritional Content (per serving):

Cal | 269.1   Fat | 10.7g   Protein |6.7g   Carbs| 26g   Fibre| 1.3g

Ingredients:

- 1 pie crust (homemade or store bought)
- 240 ml (about 1 heap cup) sugar
- 60 ml (about 1/4 cup) of cornstarch
- 1 grain (1 pinch) of salt
- 240 ml (about 1 cup) of freshly squeezed orange juice
- 125 ml (about 1/2 cup) fresh cream
- 120 ml (about 1/2 cup) of whole milk
- 4 egg yolks
- 15 grams (about 1 heap tablespoon) of finely grated orange zest
- 30 grams (2 heap tablespoons) of unsalted butter, finely diced

Directions:

1. Start by preheating your Air fryer to 180°C (350°F).
2. Spread the pie dough in a 23 cm (9 inch) pie dish and prick the bottom with a fork.
3. In a large and deep bowl, combine all together the sugar, cornstarch and salt.
4. Add in the orange juice, fresh cream, milk, egg yolks and orange zest.
5. Mix your ingredients very well until your mixture is perfectly smooth.
6. Pour your mixture over the tart crust and sprinkle with diced butter.
7. Place your tart in your air fryer and bake for about 30 to 35 minutes.
8. Remove your tart from your Air fryer and let it cool at room temperature for about 30 minutes.
9. Place your tart in the fridge for about 1 to 2 hours before serving.
10. Serve and enjoy your tart!

ALMOND TART

Servings| 4 Time|20 minutes

Nutritional Content (per serving):

Cal | 267.5   Fat | 7.3g   Protein |8.3g   Carbs| 22.8g   Fibre| 1.3g

Ingredients:

- 125 grams (about 1 heap cup) all-purpose flour
- 65 grams (about 1/2 cup) powdered sugar
- 50 grams (about 1/2 cup) of ground almonds
- 1 grain (1 pinch) of salt
- 115 grams (about 1/2 cup) of unsalted butter, softened
- 1 large egg
- 2.5 grams (about 1/2 teaspoon) of almond extract
- 100 grams (about ½ cup) of Slivered almonds to garnish

Directions:

1. Preheat your Air fryer to a temperature of about 175°C (350°F).
2. In a large and deep bowl, combine all together the flour, sugar, ground almonds and salt.
3. Add in the softened butter and mix with your fingers until you get a sandy mixture.
4. In a small deep mixing bowl, whisk all together the egg with the almond extract. Add it to the flour mixture and stir until your dough starts coming together.
5. Form a ball with the dough and spread it in a 20 cm (8 inch) tart pan.
6. Sprinkle the slivered almonds on top of your dough.
7. Place the crust in your air fryer and bake for about 15 to 20 minutes, or until the crust is golden brown and the center is set.
8. Remove your tart from your Air Fryer and set it aside to cool for a few minutes.
9. Serve and enjoy your tart!

DATES TART

Servings| 4 Time|30 minutes

Nutritional Content (per serving):

Cal | 287.3   Fat | 10.5g   Protein |11.3g   Carbs| 35g   Fibre| 1.9g

Ingredients:

- 200 grams (about 1 and 1/2 cup) of pitted and chopped dates
- 80 ml (about 1/3 cup) of boiling water
- 15 ml (about 1 heap tablespoon) of lemon juice
- 5 ml (about 1 heap teaspoon) of vanilla extract
- 80 grams (about 1/2 cup) all-purpose flour
- 80 grams (about 1/2 cup) of rolled oats
- 80 grams (about1/2 cup) brown sugar
- 2.5 grams (about 1/2 teaspoon) of baking soda
- 1.25 grams (about 1/4 teaspoon) of salt
- 60 grams (about 1/4 cup) of unsalted butter, melted

Directions:

1. In a medium and deep mixing bowl, combine all together the chopped dates, boiling water, lemon juice and vanilla extract. Set your mixture aside to sit for about 10 minutes.
2. In another medium deep bowl, combine together the all-purpose flour, rolled oats, brown sugar, baking soda and salt.
3. Add in the melted butter to your flour mixture and stir very well.
4. Divide your flour mixture into two equal parts.
5. Preheat your Air fryer to a temperature of about 180°C (350°F).
6. Place one part of the flour mixture in the bottom of an 18 cm (7 inch) diameter tart pan.
7. Spread your date mixture over the dough.
8. Sprinkle the second part of the mixture of the flour on top of the dates.
9. Bake your tart in your air fryer for about 25 to 30 minutes.
10. Allow your tart to cool before serving.
11. Serve and enjoy your tart!

WALNUT PEAR TART

Servings| 4 Time|40 minutes

Nutritional Content (per serving):

Cal| 277.6 Fat | 11.6g Protein |8.65g Carbs| 23g Fibre| 1.55g

Ingredients:

- 1 puff pastry
- 3 peeled, cored and cut into slices pears
- 80 grams (about 2/3 cup) of chopped walnuts
- 60 grams (about 1/4 cup) of powdered sugar
- 15 grams (about 1 heap tablespoon) of cornstarch
- 5 grams (about 1 heap teaspoon) of ground cinnamon
- 1.25 grams (about 1/4 teaspoon) of ground nutmeg
- 1.25 grams (about 1/4 tsp) of salt
- 15 ml (about1 tablespoon) of lemon juice
- 25 grams (about 2 heap tablespoons) of unsalted butter, melted
- 1 large egg, beaten

Directions:

1. Preheat your air fryer to a temperature of about 180° C (350° F).
2. Roll out the puff pastry on a lightly floured surface and carefully transfer to a 23 cm (9 inch) pie pan.
3. In a large and deep bowl, combine all together the pear slices, with the chopped walnuts, powdered sugar, cornstarch, cinnamon, nutmeg, salt and lemon juice.
4. Stir your ingredients very well to evenly coat the pears.
5. Pour your pear mixture over the puff pastry in your pie pan.
6. Drizzle your pears with the melted butter.
7. Brush the edge of the puff pastry with the beaten egg.
8. Bake your tart in your air fryer for about 35 to 40 minutes.
9. Remove your tart from the Air Fryer and set it aside to cool for about 5 minutes.
10. Serve and enjoy your tart!

AIR FRYER BREAD RECIPES

OLIVE BREAD

Servings| 4 Time|20 minutes

Nutritional Content (per serving):

Cal | 296   Fat | 7.3g   Protein |6g   Carbs| 16g   Fibre| 1.3g

Ingredients:

- 300 grams (about 2 and 1/2 cups) of all-purpose flour
- 7 grams (about 1 and ½ teaspoon) of instant baker's yeast
- 5 ml (about 1 heap teaspoon) of salt
- 25 grams (about 2 tablespoon) of sugar
- 185 ml (about 3/4 cup) of lukewarm water
- 60 ml (around 1/4 cup) olive oil
- 100 grams (about 3/4 cup) of pitted and chopped green olives
- 1 large beaten egg for brushing the bread (optional)

Directions:

1. In a large and deep bowl, combine all together the flour, baking powder, salt and sugar.
2. Add in the lukewarm water and olive oil; then mix until you get a smooth paste.
3. Add in the chopped olives and knead the dough for about 5 minutes.
4. Cover your dough and let it rest for about 1 hour.
5. Preheat your air fryer to a temperature of about 180°C (350°F).
6. Form the dough into a loaf shape and place it in your air fryer.
7. Brush the bread with the beaten egg, if desired.
8. Bake your prepared bread batter for about 20 minutes.
9. Remove your bread from the air fryer and set it aside to cool for a few minutes before serving.
10. Serve and enjoy your bread!

ALMOND BREAD

Servings| 4 Time|20 minutes

Nutritional Content (per serving):

Cal | 279.5   Fat | 8g   Protein |4.1g   Carbs| 18.3g   Fibre| 1g

Ingredients:

- 300 grams (about 2 and 1/2 cups) of all-purpose flour
- 7 grams (1 packet) of instant baker's yeast
- 5 grams (about 1 heap teaspoon) of salt
- 15 grams (about 1 and ½ tablespoons) of sugar
- 185 ml (around 3/4 cup) lukewarm milk
- 60 ml (about 1/4 cup) olive oil
- 100 g (1 heap cup) slivered almonds
- 1 large beaten egg for brushing the bread (optional)

Directions:

1. In a large and deep bowl, combine the flour, baking powder, salt and sugar.
2. Add in the lukewarm milk and olive oil; then mix your ingredients until they are perfectly combined.
3. Add in the slivered almonds and knead your dough for about 5 minutes.
4. Cover your dough and let it rest for about 1 hour.
5. Preheat your air fryer to a temperature of about 180°C (350°F).
6. Form your dough into a loaf shape and place it in your air fryer.
7. Brush the bread with the beaten egg.
8. Bake your prepared bread recipe for about 20 minutes.
9. Remove the bread from your air fryer and set it aside to cool for a few minutes before serving it.
10. Serve and enjoy your bread!

PUMPKIN BREAD

Servings| 3-4 Time|20 minutes

Nutritional Content (per serving):

Cal | 215.3   Fat | 11.2g   Protein |5.2g   Carbs| 19g   Fibre| 1g

Ingredients:

- 300 grams (about 2 and 1/2 cups) of all-purpose flour
- 7 grams (about 1 packet) of instant baker's yeast
- 5 grams (about 1 heap) teaspoon of salt
- 15 grams (about 1 and 1/2 teaspoons) of sugar
- 185 ml (about 3/4 cup) of pumpkin purée
- 60 ml (about 1/4 cup) of olive oil
- 1 large beaten egg for brushing the bread (optional)

Directions:

1. In a large and deep mixing bowl, combine all together the flour, baking powder, salt and sugar.
2. Add the pumpkin puree and the olive oil; then mix your ingredients very well until it becomes smooth.
3. Now, start kneading your obtained dough for a period of about 5 minutes.
4. Cover your dough and set it aside to rest for about 1 hour.
5. Preheat your air fryer to about 180°C (350°F).
6. Form your dough into a loaf shape and place it in your hot air fryer.
7. Brush the bread with the beaten egg, if desired.
8. Bake your prepared bread batter for about 20 minutes.
9. Remove the bread from your air fryer and set it aside to cool before serving for a few minutes.
10. Enjoy your bread!

MOZARELLA BREAD

Servings| 4 Time|20 minutes

Nutritional Content (per serving):

Cal | 265.3   Fat | 10.7g   Protein |7.3g   Carbs| 19g   Fibre| 0.9g

Ingredients:

- 300 grams (about 2 and 1/2 cups) of all-purpose flour
- 7 grams (about 1 packet) of instant baker's yeast
- 5 grams (about 1 heap teaspoon) of salt (5 ml)
- 20 grams (about 1 and 1/2 tablespoons) of sugar
- 185 ml (about 3/4 cup) of lukewarm water
- 60 ml (about 1/4 cup) of olive oil
- 100 grams (about 1 heap cup) of grated mozzarella
- 1 large beaten egg for brushing the bread (optional)

Directions:

1. In a large and deep mixing bowl, combine all together the flour, baking powder, salt and sugar.
2. Add in the lukewarm water and the olive oil; then mix your ingredients very well.
3. Add in the grated mozzarella and start kneading your dough for about 5 minutes.
4. Cover your dough and set it aside to rest for about 1 hour.
5. Preheat your Air fryer to a temperature of about 180°C (350°F).
6. Form your dough into a loaf shape and place it in your Air fryer.
7. Brush your bread with the beaten egg, if desired.
8. Bake your bread for about 20 minutes.
9. Remove the bread from your air fryer and set it aside to cool before serving.
10. Enjoy your bread!

RAISINS BREAD

Servings| 4 Time|20 minutes

Nutritional Content (per serving):

Cal | 266   Fat | 5.6g   Protein |5.2g   Carbs| 22g   Fibre| 0.9g

Ingredients:

- 300 grams (about 2 and 1/2 cups) all-purpose flour
- 7 grams (1 packet) of instant baker's yeast
- 5 grams (about 1 heap teaspoon) of salt
- 15 grams (about 1 heap tablespoon) of sugar
- 185 ml (about 3/4 cup) lukewarm water
- 60 ml (about 1/4 cup) olive oil
- 100 grams (about 1 heap cup) raisins
- 1 large beaten egg for brushing the bread (optional)

Directions:

1. In a large and deep bowl, combine the flour, baking powder, salt and sugar.
2. Add in the lukewarm water and olive oil; then mix very well.
3. Add in the raisins and knead your dough for about 5 minutes.
4. Cover your dough and let it rest for about 1 hour, or until it doubles in size.
5. Preheat your Air fryer to a temperature of 180° C (350° F).
6. Form your dough into a loaf shape and place it in your Air fryer.
7. Brush the bread with the beaten egg, if desired.
8. Bake your prepared bread batter for about 20 minutes.
9. Remove your bread from your air fryer and set it aside to cool for about 5 minutes.
10. Serve and enjoy your bread!

SESAME BREAD

Servings| 3-4 Time|20 minutes

Nutritional Content (per serving):

Cal | 267   Fat | 9.2g   Protein |2.1g   Carbs| 24g   Fibre| 1g

Ingredients:

- 300 grams (about 2 and 1/2 cups) all-purpose flour
- 7 grams (1 packet) of instant baker's yeast
- 5 grams (about 1 heap teaspoon) of salt
- 15 grams (about 1 heap tablespoon) of sugar
- 185 ml (about 3/4 cup) lukewarm water
- 60 ml (about 1/4 cup) olive oil
- 50 grams (about 1/4 cup) sesame seeds
- 1 large beaten egg for brushing the bread (optional)

Directions:

1. In a large and deep mixing bowl, combine flour, baking powder, salt and sugar.
2. Add in the lukewarm water and the olive oil; then mix very well.
3. Add in the sesame seeds; then knead your dough for about 5 minutes.
4. Cover your dough and asset it aside to rest for about 1 hour.
5. Preheat your air fryer to a temperature of about 180°C (350°F).
6. Form your dough into a loaf shape; then place it in your Air fryer.
7. Brush the bread with the beaten egg.
8. Sprinkle with the additional sesame seeds on top of your bread.
9. Bake your prepared bread recipe for about 20 minutes.
10. Remove the bread from your air fryer and set aside to cool before serving it.
11. Serve and enjoy your bread!

CINNAMON BREAD

Servings|4 Time|30 minutes

Nutritional Content (per serving):

Cal | 295   Fat | 10.4g   Protein |5.3g   Carbs| 24g   Fibre| 1.7g

Ingredients:

- 240 grams (2 heap cups) of all-purpose flour
- 10 grams (about 2 heap teaspoons) of baking powder
- 2.5 grams (about 1/2 teaspoon) of salt
- 2.5 grams (about 1/2 teaspoon) ground cinnamon
- 100 grams (about 1/2 cup) of sugar
- 125 ml (around 1/2 cup) of milk
- 2 large eggs
- 60 ml (about 1/4 cup) of vegetable oil
- 2 large peeled and grated apples
- 15 grams (1 heap tablespoon) of brown sugar
- 15 grams (about 1 heap tablespoon) of ground cinnamon

Directions:

1. In a large and deep mixing bowl, combine all together the flour, baking powder, salt, cinnamon and sugar.
2. In another separate deep bowl, combine all together the milk, eggs and vegetable oil.
3. Add your liquid ingredients to the rest of your dry ingredients and mix very well.
4. Add in the grated apples to your batter and mix very well.
5. In a small deep bowl, combine all together the brown sugar and the cinnamon.
6. Preheat your Air fryer to a temperature of about 180°C (350°F).
7. Pour half of your batter into a prepared greased loaf pan.
8. Sprinkle the brown sugar and the mixture of the cinnamon over your dough.
9. Pour the rest of your batter over the top and sprinkle the mixture again with the brown sugar and cinnamon.
10. Bake your recipe for a period of about 25 to 30 minutes.
11. Remove the bread from your air fryer and set it aside to cool for about 5 minutes.
12. Serve and enjoy your bread!

GARLIC BREAD

Servings| 3-4 Time|25 minutes

Nutritional Content (per serving):

Cal | 198.3   Fat | 5.7g   Protein |3.5g   Carbs | 13.6g   Fibre| 1.3g

Ingredients:

- 240 grams (about 2 heap cups) of all-purpose flour
- 10 grams (about 2 heap teaspoons) of baking powder
- 2.5 grams (about 1/2 teaspoon) of salt
- 2 cloves garlic finely chopped
- 125 ml (about 1/2 cup) of milk
- 2 large eggs
- 60 ml (about 1/4 cup) of olive oil
- 30 grams (about 2 tablespoons) of chopped fresh parsley

Directions:

1. In a large and deep mixing bowl, combine the flour, baking powder, salt and minced garlic.
2. In another deep bowl, combine the milk with the eggs and olive oil.
3. Add your liquid ingredients to your dry ingredients and mix your ingredients very well.
4. Add the chopped parsley to your batter and mix very well.
5. Preheat your Air fryer to a temperature of about 180°C (350°F).
6. Pour the prepared batter into an already prepared greased loaf pan.
7. Bake the bread batter for a period of about 25 minutes.
8. Remove the bread from your air fryer and set it aside to cool for about 5 minutes.
9. Serve and enjoy your bread!

GOAT CHEESE AND AVOCADO BREAD

Servings| 4 Time|25 minutes

Nutritional Content (per serving):

Cal | 223   Fat | 11.32g   Protein |10.9g   Carbs| 18g   Fibre| 1.9g

Ingredients:

- 240 grams (about 2 heap cups) of all-purpose flour
- 10 grams (about 2 heap teaspoons) of baking powder
- 2.5 grams (about ½ teaspoon) of salt
- 1 mashed large ripe avocado
- 60 grams (about 2 oz) of crumbled goat cheese
- 125 ml (about 1/2 cup) of milk
- 2 large eggs
- 60 ml (about 1/4 cup) of olive oil

Directions:

1. In a large and deep bowl, combine all together the flour, baking powder and the salt.
2. In another deep mixing bowl, combine the mashed avocado, crumbled goat cheese, milk, eggs and olive oil.
3. Add your liquid ingredients to your dry ingredients and mix very well.
4. Preheat your Air fryer to a temperature of about 180°C (350°F).
5. Pour your obtained bread batter into a very well-greased loaf pan.
6. Bake the prepared bread for about 20 to 25 minutes.
7. Remove your bread from your Air fryer and set it aside to cool for about 5 minutes.
8. Serve and enjoy your bread!

PISTACHIO BREAD

Servings| 4-5 Time|25 minutes

Nutritional Content (per serving):

Cal | 236   Fat | 13g   Protein |11g   Carbs| 19g   Fibre| 2.3g

Ingredients:

- 240 grams (about 2 heap cups) of all-purpose flour
- 10 grams (about 2 heap teaspoons) of baking powder
- 2.5 grams (about 1/2 teaspoon) of salt (2.5 ml)
- 60 grams (about 1/2 cup) of chopped unsalted pistachios
- 125 ml (about 1/2 cup) of milk
- 2 large eggs
- 60 ml (about 1/4 cup) olive oil

Directions:

1. In a large and deep bowl, combine all together the flour, baking powder and salt.
2. Add in the chopped pistachios and mix your ingredients very well.
3. In another deep bowl, combine the milk, eggs and the olive oil.
4. Add your liquid ingredients to your dry ingredients and mix very well.
5. Preheat your Air fryer to a temperature of about 180°C (350°F).
6. Pour your batter into a greased loaf pan.
7. Bake your prepared bread batter for a period of about 25 minutes
8. Remove the bread from your air fryer and set it aside to cool for about 5 minutes before slicing and serving it.
9. Serve and enjoy your bread!

MUFFIN AND DONUT RECIPES

CARROT WALNUT MUFFINS

Servings| 6 Time|20 minutes

Nutritional Content (per serving):

Cal | 267   Fat | 8.4g   Protein |6.3g   Carbs| 17g   Fibre| 1.2g

Ingredients:

- 200 grams (about 1 cup) of grated carrots
- 50 grams (about 1/2 cup) of chopped walnuts
- 175 grams (about 1 and 1/2 cups) all-purpose flour
- 105 grams (about 1/2 cup) granulated sugar
- 25 grams (about 2 heap tablespoons) of baking powder
- 2.5 grams (about 1/2 teaspoon) of salt
- 5 grams (about 1 heap teaspoon) of ground cinnamon
- 2 large eggs
- 85 ml (about 1/3 cup) vegetable oil
- 125 ml (about 1/2 cup) of milk
- 5 ml (about 1 heap teaspoon) of vanilla extract

Directions:

1. In a large and deep mixing bowl, combine the flour, sugar, baking powder, salt and ground cinnamon.
2. In another separate medium deep bowl, beat the eggs, vegetable oil, milk and vanilla extract.
3. Add your liquid mixture to your prepared dry mixture and mix very well until your batter is smooth.
4. Add in the grated carrots and the chopped walnuts into your batter.
5. Divide your obtained batter into about 6 muffin tins previously greased or lined with parchment paper.
6. Preheat your air fryer to 180° C (350° F) for about 5 minutes.
7. Place the muffin tins in your air fryer and bake for about 15-20 minutes.
8. Remove your muffins from your air fryer and set them aside to cool.
9. Serve and enjoy your muffins!

FIG MUFFINS

Servings| 6 Time|20 minutes

Nutritional Content (per serving):

Cal | 203   Fat | 7g   Protein |5.7g   Carbs| 24.5g   Fibre| 1.5g

Ingredients:

- 150 grams (about 1 and 1/4 cups) of all-purpose flour
- 50 grams (about 1/4 cup) of granulated sugar
- 25 grams (about 2 tablespoons) of baking powder
- 1.25 grams (about 1/4 teaspoon) of salt
- 1 large egg
- 60 ml (about 1/4 cup) vegetable oil
- 85 ml (about 1/3 cup) milk
- 5 ml (about 1 heap teaspoon) vanilla extract
- 100 grams (about 3/4 cup) dried figs, chopped
- 50 grams (about 1/2 cup) of chopped walnuts (optional)

Directions:

1. In a large and deep mixing bowl, combine all together the flour, sugar, baking powder and salt.
2. In another separate deep bowl, beat the egg, vegetable oil, milk and vanilla extract.
3. Add the liquid mixture to the dry mixture and mix very well.
4. Stir in the chopped dried figs and the chopped walnuts (optional) into your prepared batter.
5. Divide your batter into the muffin tins that are previously greased or lined with parchment paper.
6. Preheat your Air fryer to 180°C (350°F) for a period of about 5 minutes.
7. Place your muffin tins in your air fryer and bake them for about 15 to 20 minutes.
8. Remove your muffins from your Air fryer and set them aside to cool for 5 minutes.
9. Serve and enjoy your muffins!

DATES MUFFINS

Servings| 6 Time|20 minutes

Nutritional Content (per serving):

Cal | 210   Fat | 9.3g   Protein |5.9g   Carbs| 20.6g   Fibre| 1.3g

Ingredients:

- 150 grams (about 1 and 1/4 cups) of all-purpose flour
- 75 grams (about 1/3 cup) granulated sugar
- 25 grams (about 2 tablespoons) of baking powder
- 1.25 grams (about 1/4 teaspoon) of salt
- 1 large egg
- 60 ml (about 1/4 cup) vegetable oil
- 85 ml (about 1/3 cup) milk
- 5 ml (about 1 heap teaspoon) of vanilla extract
- 100 grams (about 3/4 cup) of pitted dates, chopped
- 50 grams (about 1/2 cup) of chopped walnuts (optional)

Directions:

1. In a large and deep bowl, combine the flour, sugar, baking powder and salt.
2. In another separate deep bowl, beat the egg, vegetable oil, milk and vanilla extract.
3. Add the liquid mixture to the dry mixture and mix very well.
4. Stir your chopped pitted dates and chopped walnuts (optional) into your prepared batter.
5. Divide your batter into muffin tins previously greased or lined with parchment paper.
6. Preheat your Air fryer to 180°C (350°F) for a period of about 5 minutes.
7. Place your muffin tins in your Air fryer and bake for a period of about 15-20 minutes.
8. Remove your muffins from your Air fryer and set them aside to cool for about 5 minutes.
9. Serve and enjoy your muffins!

RAISIN MUFFINS

Servings| 6 Time|20 minutes

Nutritional Content (per serving):

Cal | 275.1   Fat | 8.4g   Protein |6.2g   Carbs| 23.2g   Fibre| 1.3 g

Ingredients:

- 150 grams (about 1 and 1/4 cup) all-purpose flour
- 50 grams (about 1/4 cup) granulated sugar
- 25 grams (about 2 tablespoons) of baking powder
- 1.25 grams (about 1/4 teaspoon) of salt
- 1 large egg
- 60 ml (about 1/4 cup) vegetable oil
- 85 ml (about 1/3 cup) of milk
- 5 ml (about 1 heap teaspoon) of vanilla extract
- 100 grams (about 3/4 cup) of raisins
- 50 grams (about 1/2 cup) of chopped walnuts (optional)

Directions:

1. In a large and deep and large bowl, combine all together the flour, sugar, baking powder and salt.
2. In another deep medium bowl, beat the egg, vegetable oil, milk and vanilla extract.
3. Add your liquid mixture to your dry mixture and mix very well.
4. Stir all together the raisins and the chopped walnuts (optional) into your batter.
5. Divide your batter into your muffin tins that should be previously greased or lined with parchment paper.
6. Preheat your Air fryer to a temperature of about 180°C (350°F) for about 5 minutes.
7. Place your muffin tins in your Air fryer and bake for about 15-20 minutes.
8. Remove your muffins from your air fryer and let them cool on a wire rack.
9. Serve and enjoy your muffins!

CREAM MUFFINS

Servings| 6 Time|15 minutes

Nutritional Content (per serving):

Cal | 275   Fat | 6.5g   Protein |6.1g   Carbs| 21g   Fibre| 1.3g

Ingredients:

- 300 grams (about 2 heap cups) of all-purpose flour
- 25 grams (about 2 heap tablespoons) of baking powder
- 2.5 grams (about 1/2 teaspoon) of baking soda
- 2.5 grams (about 1/2 teaspoon) of salt
- 2 large eggs
- 200 ml (about 3/4 cup) of heavy cream
- 100 ml (about 1/3 cup + 1 tablespoon) milk
- 100 grams (about 1/2 cup) of granulated sugar
- 5 ml (about 1 heap teaspoon) of vanilla extract

Directions:

1. In a large and deep bowl, combine the flour, baking powder, baking soda and salt.
2. In another deep mixing bowl, beat the eggs, cream, milk, sugar and vanilla extract.
3. Add your liquid mixture to your dry mixture and mix very well.
4. Divide your batter into your muffin tins that are previously greased or lined with parchment paper.
5. Preheat your Air fryer to a temperature of about 180°C (350°F) for about 5 to 6 minutes.
6. Place your muffin cups in your Air fryer and bake for a period of about 12 to 15 minutes.
7. Remove your muffins from your Air fryer and set it aside to cool.
8. Serve and enjoy your muffins!

STRAWBERRY DONUTS

Servings| 6 Time|7 minutes

Nutritional Content (per serving):

Cal | 265.4   Fat | 9.5g   Protein |3.6g   Carbs| 18.3g   Fibre| 0.9g

Ingredients:

- 240 grams of flour (about 2 heap cups)
- 125 grams of sugar (about 1/2 cup)
- 10 grams (about 2 heap teaspoons) of baking powder
- 1.25 grams (about ¼ teaspoon) of salt
- 125 ml of milk (about 1/2 cup)
- 2 large eggs
- 60 grams of melted butter (about 1/4 cup)
- 5 ml (about 1 heap teaspoon) of vanilla extract
- 125 grams (about 1 heap) cup of chopped strawberries

Directions:

1. In a large and deep mixing bowl, combine the flour, sugar, baking powder and salt.
2. In another deep bowl, whisk together the milk, eggs, melted butter and vanilla extract.
3. Pour your liquid ingredients into your prepared dry ingredients and mix very well
4. Add the chopped strawberries to your obtained batter and mix very well.
5. Preheat your Air fryer to a temperature of about 190° C (375° F).
6. Lightly grease the bottom of your Air Fryer with a nonstick oil spray.
7. Using a tablespoon, scoop out one portion of the batter and gently drop it into your Air Fryer.
8. Repeat for the rest of your obtained batter, being careful not to overload your Air fryer.
9. Bake your strawberry donuts for about 5 to 7 minutes.
10. Remove your donuts from your Air fryer and set them aside to cool for about 5 minutes.
11. Sprinkle your donuts with powdered sugar.
12. Serve and enjoy your donuts!

ALMOND DONUTS

Servings|4 Time|10 minutes

Nutritional Content (per serving):

Cal | 289   Fat | 10.9g   Protein |7g   Carbs| 22.3g   Fibre| 1.8g

Ingredients:

- 240 grams (about 2 heap cups) of flour
- 100 grams (about ½ cup) of sugar
- 10 grams (about 2 heap teaspoons) of baking powder
- 1.25 grams (about ¼ teaspoon) of salt
- 125 ml of milk (about 1/2 cup)
- 2 large eggs
- 60 grams (about ¼ cup) of melted butter
- 5 ml (about 1 heap teaspoon) of almond extract
- 60 grams (about ½ cup) of slivered almonds

Directions:

1. In a large and deep mixing bowl, combine the flour, sugar, baking powder and salt.
2. In another deep bowl, whisk together the milk, eggs, melted butter and almond extract.
3. Pour your liquid ingredients into your dry ingredients and mix your ingredients very well.
4. Add your slivered almonds to your batter and mix very well.
5. Preheat your Air fryer to a temperature of about 190° C (375° F).
6. Lightly grease the bottom of your Air fryer with some nonstick oil spray.
7. Using a tablespoon, scoop out a portion of your dough and form a small hole in the center using your finger.
8. Carefully drop your donut into your Air fryer and repeat for the rest of the dough, being careful not to overload your Air fryer.
9. Bake your formed donuts for about 5 to 7 minutes.
10. Remove your donuts from your Air fryer and set aside to cool for about 5 minutes.
11. To coat the Air fried donuts with almonds, put the slivered almonds in a deep plate; then dip each donut in the almond mixture to coat very well.
12. Sprinkle some powdered sugar on top of your donuts.
13. Serve and enjoy your donuts!

MATCHA GREEN TEA DONUTS

Servings| 4Time|7 minutes

Nutritional Content (per serving):

Cal | 206.2   Fat | 7.5g   Protein |4g   Carbs| 14g   Fibre| 1g

Ingredients:

- 240grams flour (about ½ pounds)
- 100grams (about ½ cup) of sugar (1/2 cup)
- 10 grams (about 2 heap teaspoons) of baking powder
- 1.25 grams (about 1/4 teaspoon) of salt
- 25 grams (about 2 heap tablespoons) of matcha green tea powder
- 125ml (about ½ cup) of milk
- 2 large eggs
- 60grams (about ¼ cup) of melted butter

To prepare the matcha green tea frosting:
- 125 grams (about 1 heap cup) of powdered sugar
- 15 grams (about 1 heap tablespoon) of matcha green tea powder
- 45 ml (about 3 heap tablespoons) of milk

Directions:

1. In a large and deep mixing bowl, combine the flour, sugar, baking powder, salt and matcha green tea.
2. In another medium mixing bowl, whisk together the milk, eggs and melted butter.
3. Pour your liquid ingredients into your dry ingredients and mix very well.
4. Preheat your Air fryer to a temperature of about 190°C (375°F).
5. Lightly grease the bottom of your fryer with nonstick oil spray.
6. Using a tablespoon, scoop out a portion of your dough and form a small hole in the center with your finger.
7. Carefully and gently drop your donuts into your Air Fryer and repeat the same process for the rest of your dough.
8. Bake your donuts for about 5 to 7 minutes.
9. Remove your donuts from your Air Fryer and drain them on a sheet of paper towel.

Frosting Instructions:

1. In a large mixing bowl, combine powdered sugar and matcha green tea.
2. Slowly add in the milk while mixing very well
3. Dip each of the donuts in the prepared glaze and set aside to drain on a cooling rack for about 5 to 10 minutes.
4. Serve and enjoy your donuts!

COCONUT DONUTS

Servings| 6 Time|7 minutes

Nutritional Content (per serving):

Cal | 225   Fat | 10.7g   Protein |8.5g   Carbs| 17.8g   Fibre| 1 g

Ingredients:

- 240grams (about 2 heap cups) of flour
- 100grams (about ½ cup) of sugar
- 10 grams (about 2 heap teaspoons) of baking powder
- 1.25 grams (about 1/4 teaspoon) of salt
- 60grams (about ½ cup) of shredded coconut
- 125ml (about ½ cup) of milk
- 2 large eggs
- 60grams (about ¼ cup) of melted butter
- 2.5 ml (about 1/2 teaspoon) of vanilla extract

For the coconut icing:
- 125 grams (about 1 cup) of icing sugar
- 125 grams (about 1/2 cup) of shredded coconut
- 2 to 3 tablespoons of milk

Directions:

1. In a large and deep bowl, combine the flour, sugar, baking powder, salt and grated coconut.
2. In another mixing deep bowl, whisk together the milk, eggs, melted butter and vanilla extract.
3. Pour your liquid ingredients into the dry ingredients and mix very well.
4. Preheat your Air fryer to a temperature of about 190° C (375° F).
5. Lightly grease the bottom of your Air fryer with nonstick oil spray.
6. Using a tablespoon, scoop out a portion of the dough and form a small hole in the center with your finger.
7. Carefully and gently drop the donut into your Air fryer and repeat for the rest of the dough.
8. Bake the obtained donuts for about 5 to 7 minutes.
9. Remove your donuts from your Air fryer and drain them on a sheet of paper towel.
10. In a large deep bowl, mix the icing sugar and the grated coconut.
11. Slowly add in the milk while mixing very well to obtain a smooth and thick icing.
12. Dip each of the donuts in the glaze and let dry on a cooling rack for about 5 to 10 minutes.
13. Serve and enjoy your donuts!

BLUBERRY DONUTS

Servings| 5-6 Time|10 minutes

Nutritional Content (per serving):

Cal | 247   Fat | 14g   Protein |10.5g   Carbs| 22.5g   Fibre| 1.3g

Ingredients:

- 190grams (about 1 ½ cups) of all-purpose flour (1 1/2 cups)
- 50grams (1/4 cup) of granulated sugar
- 10 grams (about 2 teaspoons) of baking powder
- 1.25 grams (about 1/4 teaspoon) of salt
- 1 large egg
- 125ml milk (about 1/2 cup)
- 30ml (about 2 tablespoons) of vegetable oil
- 2.5 ml (about 1/2 teaspoon) of vanilla extract
- 125grams (about 1 heap cup) of fresh blueberries

Directions:

1. In a large and deep mixing bowl, combine all together the flour, sugar, baking powder and salt.
2. In another mixing bowl, beat all together the egg then add in the milk, vegetable oil and vanilla extract. Mix your ingredients very well.
3. Add your liquid ingredients to your dry ingredients and mix very well
4. Add the fresh blueberries to your batter and mix in a gentle way.
5. Preheat your Air fryer to a temperature of about 190° C (375° F).
6. Lightly spray the bottom of your Air fryer with nonstick oil spray.
7. Fill each cavity of the donut pan about two-thirds full with the prepared batter.
8. Bake your donuts for about 8 to 10 minutes
9. Remove your donuts from your Air fryer and let cool for a few minutes before serving
10. Serve and enjoy your donuts!

WHOLE WHEAT DONUTS

Servings| 6 Time|10 minutes

Nutritional Content (per serving):

Cal | 210   Fat | 8g   Protein |6.9g   Carbs| 19.3g   Fibre| 2g

Ingredients:

- 200grams of whole wheat flour (1 and 1/2 cups)
- 50 grams (about 1/4 cup) of granulated sugar
- 10 grams (about 2 heap teaspoons) baking powder
- 1.25 grams (about ¼ teaspoon) of baking soda
- 1.25 grams (about 1/4 teaspoon) salt
- 125ml (about ½ cup) of skimmed milk
- 2 large eggs
- 30 ml (about 2 heap tablespoons) of vegetable oil
- 5 ml (about 1 heap teaspoon) of vanilla extract

Directions:

1. In a large and deep mixing bowl, combine whole wheat flour, sugar, baking powder, baking soda and salt.
2. In another medium deep bowl, beat all together the eggs then add in the milk, vegetable oil and the vanilla extract. Mix your ingredients very well.
3. Add your liquid ingredients to your dry ingredients and mix very well
4. Preheat your Air fryer to a temperature of about 190° C (375° F).
5. Lightly spray the bottom of your Air fryer with nonstick oil spray.
6. Fill each cavity of your donut pan two-thirds full with batter.
7. Bake the prepared donuts for about 8 to 10 minutes
8. Remove the donuts from your Air fryer and set them to cool for a few minutes before serving.
9. Serve and enjoy your donuts!

THANKS FOR READING

Thank you for choosing our Air Fryer Baking Cookbook! We hope our recipes have inspired you to explore the world of healthier and easier baking.

If you enjoyed using our cookbook, we would be grateful if you could leave a review. Your feedback helps us improve our cookbooks and helps others make an informed decision when choosing their next cookbook.

Thank you for your support and for being a part of our air fryer baking community. We can't wait to hear about your cooking adventures and see photos of your delicious creations.

Enjoy your crispy and delicious treats, and happy air frying!

Printed in Great Britain
by Amazon